THE ESSENTIAL SARMIENTO

*Civilization, Barbarism,
and Progress*

THE ESSENTIAL SARMIENTO

Civilization, Barbarism, and Progress

Edited by William Acree

Translations by John Charles Chasteen

With an Introduction by Oscar Chamosa

Hackett Publishing Company, Inc.
Indianapolis/Cambridge

Copyright © 2025 by Hackett Publishing Company, Inc.

All rights reserved
Printed in the United States of America

28 27 26 25   1 2 3 4 5 6 7

For further information, please address
  Hackett Publishing Company, Inc.
  P.O. Box 44937
  Indianapolis, Indiana 46244-0937

  www.hackettpublishing.com

Cover and interior design by E. L. Wilson
Composition by Aptara, Inc.

Cataloging-in-Publication data can be accessed via the Library of Congress Online Catalog.

Library of Congress Control Number: 2024943882

ISBN-13: 978-1-64792-213-9 (pbk.)
ISBN-13: 978-1-64792-214-6 (PDF ebook)
ISBN-13: 978-1-64792-215-3 (epub)

The paper used in this publication meets the minimum requirements of American National Standard for Information Sciences—Permanence of Paper for Printed Library Materials, ANSI Z39.48–1984.

∞

CONTENTS

Preface: *The Alexander Hamilton of Latin America*   vii
   William Acree

Introduction: *Work in Progress: Nineteenth-Century Argentina
and Domingo Sarmiento*   xiii
   Oscar Chamosa

Further Readings   xxix
Chronology   xxxi
Maps of Argentina & Latin America   xxxiii

1. ***Facundo*: The Shaping of a Paradigm**   1

    Introduction   2

    Chapter 1: Physical Geography and Its Impact on the Argentine Republic   5

    Chapter 2: The Argentine National Character and Its Originality   14

    Chapter 3: Argentine Sociability: The *Pulpería*   23

    Chapter 5: The Life of Juan Facundo Quiroga   28

    Final Considerations (Two passages from later chapters of *Facundo*)   37

2. ***Facundo*'s Impact**   42

    "My Books," from *Recuerdos de Provincia*, first published in 1850   42

    "On the Appearance of *Facundo* in Italian Translation," in *El Nacional*, 22 September 1881   44

    "The Case of Camila O'Gorman," in *Crónica* [Santiago, Chile], 26 August 1849   45

3. ***El Chacho*: The Last of a Breed**   51

Contents

4. Immigration and the Expanding Frontier   **58**

"Immigration," in *El Nacional*, 25 July 1855   58

"Organized Settlement Projects," in *El Nacional*,
8 August 1878   62

"The Indians," in *El Nacional*, 2 November 1879   65

"The Campaign against the Indians," in *El Nacional*,
22 February 1879   67

"Naturalizing the Millions," in *El Diario*, 16 November 1887   70

5. Civilization in Daily Life   **75**

"On Reading Newspapers," in *El Mercurio*, 4 July and
7 August 1841   76

"On Theater and Cultural Criticism," in *El Mercurio*,
8 November 1841   79

"Christmas Eve Celebrations," in *El Mercurio*,
26 December 1841   80

"The Theater, a Tool of Cultural Education," in *El Mercurio*,
20 June 1842   83

"Goodbye to Carnival!" in *El Mercurio*, 10 February 1842   86

"Carnival of 1857," in *El Nacional*, 25 February 1857   90

"The Railroad Linking Buenos Aires to San Fernando:
A Public Address Delivered 17 August 1859"   93

"Rustic Capital," *Annals of Education*, 1858   96

"Educating Women"   100

Selection from "North and South America.
A Discourse Delivered before the Rhode-Island
Historical Society," 27 December 1865   102

6. Sarmiento the National Hero   **104**

Funerary Honors for Sarmiento, 21 September 1888   104

Index   107

PREFACE

The Alexander Hamilton of Latin America

William Acree

Born in the rural northwest of Argentina to a family of scarce economic means, Domingo Faustino Sarmiento (1811–1888) became one of the most towering figures in Latin American history. Like Alexander Hamilton, as the refrain from the Broadway show tells us, Sarmiento wrote like he was running out of time. In fact, his complete writings fill fifty-two volumes, each containing hundreds of pages—production on a scale that far exceeded that of many of his fellow statesmen of letters combined. Looking at Sarmiento's complete works on any library shelf can be awe-inspiring, especially if we think about a single person writing so much in a lifetime, more than a century before the existence of the computer technology we now regularly use to write.

Like Hamilton, Sarmiento was an emigrant (exiled from his native Argentina for many years), a soldier, a diplomat, a statesman, and a person whose mind and pen were never at rest. Like Hamilton's, Sarmiento's life and work existed parallel and in relation to the emergence of a new nation, with all its political upheavals. Both men were nation builders at moments when these communities were taking shape out of the colonial framework. Both designed institutions that would be critical for each nation's future—Hamilton the US treasury, Sarmiento Argentina's public education system. Both occupied several government positions, Sarmiento in Chile and in Argentina, where he served one term as president. Both tended to exemplify a conservative brand of nineteenth-century liberalism. And, like Hamilton, Sarmiento chased honor and fame, seeking through writing to make his voice and ideas omnipresent.

The similarities between Hamilton and Sarmiento could go on. But there is one important distinction between the two. In contrast to Hamilton, whose memory was largely relegated to his image on the US ten-dollar bill until Lin-Manuel Miranda's *Hamilton* made his name, story, and songs common currency around the world, Domingo Sarmiento's memory, legacy, and impacts have been constants in Argentina since the 1800s—in addition to his presence on the fifty-peso bill. As Oscar Chamosa relates in his Introduction to this volume, Sarmiento exercised outsize influence in debates between Argentina's new political parties; in the design and building of Argentina's regional and national institutions; among diplomatic and intellectual circles in Chile, Uruguay, and elsewhere throughout Latin America and the United States; in the expanding world of letters; and as the chief architect of the public primary education system in Argentina, which, thanks to its rapid implementation in the 1880s and 1890s, made the country one of the most literate in the world by the beginning of the twentieth century. Simply put, through the education system, the daily exchanges of currency with his likeness, the presence of reading as a feature of national identity, and the sharp divide in attitudes between urban residents and the rural countryside, Sarmiento's shadow is hard to escape.

In other areas of Latin America as well as in the United States and Europe, Sarmiento is best known for *Facundo*, an 1845 diatribe against the government of the caudillo strongman Juan Manuel de Rosas. Part biography of Rosas's fellow caudillo Facundo Quiroga, part social portrait of contemporary Argentina, Sarmiento's *Facundo* is one of the most influential essays ever written about Latin America. *Civilization and Barbarism*, the subtitle of the book, presents a dichotomy between things urban and European on the one hand and things rural and native to Latin America on the other. Things urban and European were civilized and to be encouraged. Things rural and native were barbarous and to be eliminated. Sarmiento did not invent the dichotomy. To the contrary, it loomed over nineteenth-century Latin America as a master interpretive paradigm even before he wrote. But *Facundo* was to become its primary statement, and Sarmiento its best-known exponent. Translated into multiple languages soon after its initial publication in the Chilean press, the essay became a true best seller, leading some of Sarmiento's like-minded contemporaries to talk of reading the book in one sitting and how, according to the one-time Argentine president Nicolás Avellaneda, the book "lit up the night like a shooting star."

Sarmiento's vision of civilization was not without critique. In fact, toward the last third of the century, many politicians and intellectuals celebrated American republics as superior to European nations, where monarchy continued to dominate state affairs. One of the best-known examples was José Martí, one of Cuba's "founding fathers," whose widely influential essay "Our América" exuded pride in everything American and cast disdain on those who continued turning to Europe for inspiration.

Preface

But even in the face of these shifting ideological winds, Sarmiento's famous dichotomy remained a model for understanding Argentine and Latin American experiences throughout much of the twentieth century.

So when students learn about the clash between civilization and barbarism in Latin American history, the go-to source is Sarmiento. Yet while *Facundo* has been Sarmiento's most celebrated, despised, and cited piece, and though selections from the essay constitute a central part of this reader, recall the other fifty-one volumes he wrote! In fact, it was *after* the publication of *Facundo* that Sarmiento became one of Argentina's most vocal and influential public figures. For close to half a century, until his death in 1888, he wrote tirelessly, garnering the nickname of *caudillo* of the press, while occupying a range of government positions. It may not come as a surprise, then, that at Sarmiento's funeral the Argentine president at the time proclaimed: "Now he belongs to the ages. And when our Argentine Republic eventually takes its place at last among the leading nations of the globe, its sons and daughters can look back at those winking stars in the firmament and recognize there the profile of Sarmiento, consecrated now for all time as a Founding Father."

The Essential Sarmiento captures core examples of this extensive activity, bringing together the most engaging chapters of *Facundo* with other rich materials of equal interest. Sarmiento's newspaper columns, other books, correspondence with contemporaries, and blueprints for national projects gathered here provide the reader with glimpses into issues of public education, the emerging contours of liberalism, and the social values of activities like theater and carnival, among others, as central to civilization, barbarism, and progress. Few of these other writings had been translated into English before this, despite the valuable perspectives they yield on how Sarmiento's notions of civilization and barbarism developed over close to five decades of writing and public life. Now, these selections can facilitate explorations of the civilization-barbarism conversation as it played out after Juan Manuel de Rosas left power in the early 1850s. Readers will be able to compare Sarmiento's views of the countryside and caudillos in *Facundo* with the later portrait of El Chacho, one of the region's last gaucho caudillos. Columns that Sarmiento wrote on the significance of reading and the role of theater, daily play, and carnival in instilling civilized behavior offer students a variety of perspectives for understanding changing notions of morality and how they were linked to economic success. Similarly, samples of writings on the expansion of the rail system and the roles of immigrants in literally shaping the future of the country's demographic and moral character provide important

Preface

views into what Sarmiento thought was necessary for Argentina (and other Latin American countries) to achieve progress and be considered a modern nation.

The Essential Sarmiento, then, offers a concise though simultaneously inclusive collection of the writings of the Alexander Hamilton of Latin America. Here readers will find:

- Attitudes that raise questions about race and nation building in Latin America; the weight of international sources of inspiration; and tensions between local, regional, and global forces
- Combinations of biting critique with hints of awe or reverence or pleasant surprise, whether the focus is Christmas Eve revelries or the strength and skills of rural cattle rustlers
- An emphasis on "social betterment"—the idea of national customs and behaviors would become more refined through demographic "improvement"
- The belief that the "forces of nature" that so define the Argentine countryside, in Sarmiento's assessment, permeate all aspects of life in the country
- Contradictions that emerge over time
- A selection of writings that pose many questions about national immigration policy; why certain ideas that Sarmiento cultivated or developed during his life have had such staying power; what to make of his praise for elements of rural life that stand in the way of his vision of progress; and what it meant for Sarmiento and fellow policymakers to radically shift their position on immigration and related issues

These areas as well as others that come into focus for readers will surely raise questions that can lead to enriching conversations and reflections. Sarmiento's thinking, like his life, is full of twists, turns, and complexities that can confound. With Oscar Chamosa's Introduction to Sarmiento's life and its connections to the early history of the new nation of Argentina in the 1800s, and through John Chasteen's expertly crafted and engaging translations, *The Essential Sarmiento* aims to help readers explore these complexities and the insights they can yield for a deeper understanding of Latin America since independence.

As readers will see, Sarmiento's thinking went far beyond the heat of the partisan clashes captured in *Facundo*, informing debates on international

Preface

trade, fashion, education, immigration—you name it—in ways that long outlived Sarmiento himself and reached far beyond Argentina.

Alas, there is not—yet—a musical that takes up the many stories of Sarmiento's life. But across Argentina, streets and subway stations are named after him, while busts of the statesman peer over squares from north to south and his portrait hangs in schoolrooms throughout the country. His memory is invoked regularly in initiatives that praise or chastise the legacy of his work. And the ideas that he put to paper like he was running out of time continue to loom large in public and political life in Argentina and elsewhere in Latin America. That's precisely why the collection of readings gathered here hopes to give a sense of the essential Sarmiento.

Contributors

William Acree is Professor of Spanish, American Culture Studies, and Performing Arts at Washington University in St. Louis. He is the author of *Staging Frontiers: The Making of Modern Popular Culture in Argentina and Uruguay* and *Everyday Reading: Print Culture & Collective Identity in Argentina and Uruguay, 1780–1910*. His edited volumes include *The Gaucho Juan Moreira: True Crime in Nineteenth-Century Argentina*. Acree currently serves as the Vice Dean of Interdisciplinary Initiatives and Innovation in Arts & Sciences at WashU.

John Charles Chasteen is a translator and Professor emeritus of Latin American History at the University of North Carolina, Chapel Hill. His many published translations include *The Gaucho Juan Moreira: True Crime in Nineteenth-Century Argentina*; *The Vortex: A Novel*; *The Alienist and Other Stories of Nineteenth-Century Brazil*; and *Santa: A Novel of Mexico City*, as well as numerous nonfiction titles. His most recent book is *After Eden: A Short History of the World*.

Oscar Chamosa is Associate Professor of History at the University of Georgia. He is the author of *The Argentine Folklore Movement: Sugar Elites, Criollo Workers and the Politics of Cultural Nationalism, 1900–1955*. He also co-edited with Matthew Karush *The New Cultural History of Peronism: Power & Identity in Mid-Twentieth Century Argentina*. Chamosa has published several book chapters and journal articles in English and Spanish. His latest book is *Building on Trust, Faith, and Power: Habitat for Humanity's Networks from Southwest Georgia to the Maya Highlands of Guatemala*.

INTRODUCTION

WORK IN PROGRESS: NINETEENTH-CENTURY ARGENTINA AND DOMINGO SARMIENTO

Oscar Chamosa

Domingo Faustino Sarmiento, the author of *Facundo*, was president of Argentina from 1868 to 1874. This was supposed to be the pinnacle of a long, multifaceted career that included military, diplomatic, ministerial, journalistic, and educational appointments. The most indelible mark that Sarmiento left was on the Argentine public education system, which he built and nurtured through the different offices he occupied from 1853 on. Yet despite his extended political résumé, what defined Sarmiento's life was his writing. Daily, he wrote pages and pages of essays, memoirs, newspaper columns, and personal letters. Paraphrasing Lin Manuel Miranda, Sarmiento wrote as if he was running out of time. And just like the fictionalized Federalist leader Hamilton, Sarmiento tried to write a nation into existence. Or, perhaps, it was Argentina that wrote Sarmiento's life?

In a fortunate coincidence, Sarmiento was born precisely nine months after the Revolution of May 25, 1810, the first step toward the independence of the Río de la Plata provinces. That means that Sarmiento was conceived at the same time as his country. The country, first called the United Provinces of the Río de la Plata, had a more extended gestation period, however. The patriots that broke with Spain did not declare independence until 1816. Moreover, the Spaniards did not surrender until 1824.

The Argentine general José de San Martín planned to cross the Andes and join revolutionaries in Chile and Peru to defeat the Royal Spanish army in their Peruvian stronghold and consolidate the fragile freedom. For that purpose, the general recruited and trained an army in Cuyo, the region bordering the Andes, including the provinces of Mendoza, San Luis, and San Juan. The last one was Sarmiento's hometown. When the methodical San Martín mobilized all the region's resources to cross the Andes with his army, Sarmiento was a bright six-year-old, perfectly aware

Introduction

of the excitement around him. When San Martín marched through the city of San Juan on his way to Chile, Sarmiento's father, many family members, and neighbors were among the soldiers. After the decisive victory over the Spaniards in Maipo, Chile, San Martín's army and Chilean units sailed to Peru. Sarmiento's old man, meanwhile, returned to his trade of driving cattle from Chile to San Juan, over the same forbidding mountain passes the army had marched through. It is easy to imagine the young Sarmiento itching to be a part of the epic struggle taking place across the Andes. The War of Independence ended on December 9, 1824, when a combined army of five future South American nations led by General José Antonio de Sucre defeated the last Spanish holdout in Ayacucho, in the Peruvian Andes.

As the independence campaign unfolded, the Río de la Plata government collapsed. Paraguay had already declared its independence from both Spain and Buenos Aires. The Alto Peru resisted Buenos Aires's armies for fourteen years. When it became independent, it took a new name, Bolivia, from its liberator, the Venezuelan Simón Bolívar. More dangerous for Buenos Aires was the Portuguese invasion of the Río de la Plata's Banda Oriental (the Eastern Bank). After Brazilian independence in 1822, Emperor Pedro I decided to keep the Banda Oriental within his possessions. Once Paraguay and Bolivia parted ways, and with the future Uruguay occupied by Brazil, the United Provinces no longer merited that name.

In 1819, an interprovincial Congress was convened in Buenos Aires and drafted a constitution for the United Provinces of South America, but the union lasted only a few months. A new congress was convened in Buenos Aires by request of the Buenos Aires provincial government in 1825. The rationale for this second constitutional attempt was to regroup the local militias into a national army that could withstand the Brazilian advance in the Banda Oriental. The war with the imperial neighbor began a year later and lasted until the end of 1828. Sarmiento followed these events from afar, in the relative isolation of his landlocked province. He was already of age to become an aspiring officer, as expected from a young man of his rank. But his primary goal was to get a higher education. Sarmiento had two options: the enlightened University of Buenos Aires or the priestly University of Córdoba. He failed admission to the former and refused to attend the latter. Thus, the future champion of South American public education continued to be homeschooled.

In 1824, the National Congress appointed Bernardino Rivadavia as the first president of the Argentine Republic. Like many fellow early

Introduction

Latin American leaders, Rivadavia was an enlightened reformer who aspired to modernize his country through political stability, foreign trade, and religious tolerance. Like other liberal leaders of his time, he thought the Catholic Church was the main obstacle to the country's progress; thus, his government proceeded to eliminate convents and secularize ecclesiastical properties. Rivadavia and his allies thought that the provinces, dominated by landowners and priests, were not ready to take the path of modernity and, therefore, should be ruled by the national government. Followers of this platform called themselves Unitarians (*Unitarios*). Controlling the Congress, the Unitarian party passed the Constitution of 1826, which gave the national government authority to appoint governors and manage the provinces' natural resources. Seven hundred miles from the center of the action, the teenage Sarmiento devoured any news that arrived from Buenos Aires (often via Valparaiso, Chile). He and his family endorsed Rivadavia's liberal plans. Alas, the liberal dreams crashed against the reality of the war with Brazil, which exhausted the government finances even as it failed to deliver a decisive victory. In 1828, Brazil and Argentina recognized the disputed territory as the independent nation of Uruguay. Argentina was also a relatively new name, officially replacing the United Provinces of the Río de la Plata in 1826. However, two years later, Argentina was only a geographical expression (much like what Prince Metternich said of Italy). Supporters of provincial rights, who called themselves Federalists (*Federales*), withdrew their support from the National Congress and the provinces resumed their autonomy. As Sarmiento came of age, his country disintegrated. It would take three decades to put it back together, the time that Sarmiento took to become its president.

The 1828–1830 Unitarian/Federal war prompted Argentina's collapse, but the problem had roots in the post-independence reconfiguration of the regional economies. With the end of Spanish rule and the partial closure of the Potosí silver mines, the only remaining profitable business in the Río de la Plata region was trading cow hides, beef jerky, and other cattle byproducts. British merchants were happy to buy these staples at the price they saw fit. The hide and dried beef trade cycle lasted until the late 1840s; during that time, large cattle owners, or *estancieros* in local parlance, dominated the provincial economy and politics, displacing the old urban elite of merchants, lawyers, and regular army officers.

Since the colonial period, the *estancieros*, often the uncouth cousins of wealthy city merchants, had officiated as rural authorities. The *estancieros*'

Introduction

public duties included officiating as judges, forming and maintaining the rural militia, protecting their districts against Indigenous raids, preventing internal disorder, and recruiting for the regular army in case of foreign conflict. After independence, with the national armies depleted and the political legitimacy of the urban elites shattered, these rural militias were now the only forces still capable of imposing a measure of order. The *estancieros* traded their cattle for political ascendancy, buying their militiamen's loyalty and settling disputes with fellow ranchers. In the crisis of the 1820s, most *estancieros* understood that their best interests lay on the side of the Federal party. Buying up provincial legislatures was easier than controlling a national congress with access to foreign credit. The urbane Unitarians disparaged these political *estancieros*, calling them *caudillos*, a Spanish term popularized during the Napoleonic wars that denoted informal authority or leadership of a small armed group. The Unitarians also gave the name of *gaucho* to the caudillos' followers.

In the first half of the nineteenth century, *gaucho* meant "rustler" or "outlaw." As the nineteenth century progressed and the ranching economy became better funded and more regulated, however, the term lost that initial connotation. *Gaucho* came to designate the Argentine cowboys and, by extension, any rural inhabitant of the Pampas. Nevertheless, the confusion remained. Later in the century, writers such as José Hernández, Eduardo Gutiérrez, and the British-Argentine W. H. Hudson created a popular literary genre in which gaucho desperadoes and gaucho heroes overlapped, adding complexity to the term while also associating it with the essence of Argentine nationality.

Back in 1835, however, while writing *Facundo* in his Chilean exile, Sarmiento consistently associated the words *caudillo* and *gaucho* with barbarism, political and otherwise. When Sarmiento called for an end to the "gaucho problem," he was bemoaning the rural lawlessness he saw as the root of caudillo rule. At this stage of his thought, Sarmiento theorized that the gauchos' barbarity resulted from the empty landscape they inhabited rather than from their race. The constant presence of the horizon, the solitude, and the dangers lurking behind each thicket infused in the gaucho a disregard for social mores and any other justice than the edge of his long knife. Some noted that Sarmiento's geographic determinism was more literary than sociological: Sarmiento's gauchos resembled the feral manhood of Sir Walter Scott's highlanders, James Fenimore Cooper's backwoodsmen, or Lord Byron's Balkan long riders. But to credit Sarmiento's power of observation, the landscape or perhaps, more correctly, location and natural resources, did define power

Introduction

distribution in post-colonial Argentina. The eastern riverine provinces, with easier access to foreign markets and tender pastures, made their caudillos rich and powerful. That is why Juan Manuel de Rosas, the most prominent rancher and the governor of Buenos Aires Province, was the dominant figure in Argentina for over twenty years. The caudillos Estanislao López of Santa Fe and Francisco Ramírez of Entre Ríos enjoyed advantages second only to those of Buenos Aires. In 1830, Rosas, López, and Ramírez signed the first of a series of pacts that made up for the lack of a constitution and a national state. Farther from the coast, the caudillos of interior provinces lacked the wealth and stability of their eastern colleagues. Their relative poverty made them a target for internal intrigues and interprovincial challenges. The strength of these caudillos depended on the favor of the self-sufficient eastern caudillos.

If fodder and ports were the props of caudillo autonomy, the leaders of San Juan could have little hope of keeping their province free from outside interference. Sarmiento's home province was one of the most isolated, arid, and underpopulated jurisdictions in the shattered Argentine Republic. Most of the population lived in the San Juan River valley, a perfect place for growing Malbec grapes, but not for sustaining ranching. (In the 1800s, the San Juan wine industry remained in an unforeseeable future.) Outside that oasis extends a moonscape of barren valleys and rocky mountain slopes. In the colonial era, gold mining allowed a few San Juan families to live above the rest. Sarmiento's family did not belong to the wealthy miners—his father, as mentioned, was a cattle driver, and his mother a weaver. But by name, the Sarmiento-Albarracíns belonged to the small group of families that made up the San Juan middling elite of officeholders, clerics, and traders. This elite had decisively supported the cause of independence and liberal reforms. For Sarmiento, the San Juan Valley was a beacon of civilization shining over the windblown desert of the eastern Andean piedmont. Yet, during the nineteenth century, Federal caudillos invaded San Juan several times, humiliating the proud local elite and imposing onerous conditions.

These caudillos and their gauchos came not from the faraway pampas but from the nearby llanos, or flatlands, of La Rioja Province. The llanos are a range of scrubland and salt flats extending like a no-man's-land among Córdoba, Catamarca, La Rioja, San Juan, and San Luis provinces. Perhaps because none of these provinces showed interest, La Rioja claimed provincial sovereignty over the thorny basin. The lack of surface water made it inconvenient for human habitation. But the few entrepreneurs that owned the rare *pozos*, or springs, could extract some profit from raising cattle and feeding the passing herds that gauchos drove between the provinces.

The most powerful rancher in the llanos was Juan Facundo Quiroga, La Rioja's militia captain and Sarmiento's ticket to literary fame. Quiroga was related to the traditional families of La Rioja and San Juan but grew up in the llanos. His rise to power seemed to follow the classic script of the overlooked country bumpkin who outmaneuvers his smartly dressed city cousins. Furthermore, with his large, penetrating eyes, matted black hair, brushy sideburns, and smug smile, Quiroga perfectly fulfilled the stereotypical physique of the nineteenth-century Latin American caudillo. Like most caudillos, past and present, his activities blurred the boundaries between legal business, politics, and plunder. In 1823, a failed bid over a silver mine in La Rioja put him at odds with Bernardino Rivadavia and his La Rioja allies. Quiroga embraced the Federal party and singlehandedly thwarted the Unitarians' attempts to pass a national constitution. From 1824 to 1826, in a series of swift attacks, Quiroga's gauchos occupied Tucumán, Catamarca, and San Juan, purging the Unitarian factions, imposing his minions, and establishing a solid reputation as an invincible field commander.

In December 1828, with the debacle of the national government and the ensuing civil war, Quiroga faced the advance of the veteran regular army that returned from Brazil holding the Unitarian banner. The Unitarians defeated Quiroga in two key battles and forced him to find refuge in Buenos Aires, where Rosas had crushed the Unitarian faction. In the interior, Quiroga's defeat prompted a Unitarian spring. Sarmiento, then a twenty-year-old rural teacher, joined the Unitarian army, hoping to contribute to what he saw as the civilizational cause. The spring lasted for two years. In 1831, Quiroga returned with his unstoppable gaucho cavalry, reinforced with Rosas's supplies, to reinstate Federal rule. For Sarmiento, it was time for exile, his first, in Chile. After defeating the Unitarians, Quiroga became Rosas's surrogate, mediating in the constant internecine feuds among Federal caudillos. His arbitrations did not leave everyone happy. On February 15, 1835, hired hands fatally shot Quiroga as he traveled from Córdoba to Santiago del Estero. The Reinafé brothers, a triad of caudillos who ruled Córdoba, were charged with being the intellectual authors of the crime. Using an untested prerogative, Rosas ordered the apprehension, extradition, and public execution of the three caudillos, along with the material authors, in Buenos Aires. Then, the terrible ghost of Quiroga, whom Sarmiento invokes in the opening sentence of his *Facundo*, would be able to rest in peace. Rosas used Quiroga's tragic

Introduction

end to increase his ascendancy over the provinces and justify the repression of his political enemies. After Quiroga, no caudillo could occupy a gubernatorial seat without Rosas's consent.

Rosas's government was still not the tyranny that Sarmiento so powerfully denounces in *Facundo*, however. In the peaceful year of 1837, Sarmiento returned from Chile to San Juan, where he founded a newspaper and returned to political criticism. In Buenos Aires, poets, essayists, and dilettantes from different provinces met at fancy literary soirees. They listened to world travelers, discussed the fashions of European romantic art, and plotted to overcome the Federal–Unitarian dichotomy. The young writers in this group were dubbed the Generation of 1837. The most talented of the group, Esteban Echeverría, wrote the hit short story "The Slaughterhouse," an elitist but gripping description of a typical day in the Buenos Aires cattle yards. Another member of the Generation of 1837, Juan Bautista Alberdi, from Tucumán Province, was the future father of the Argentine constitution and Sarmiento's rival. In 1839, however, a Unitarian military uprising poisoned the air across the Argentine confederation. Rosas imposed martial law and put a long list of citizens under surveillance. Nighttime shootings at doors and windows drove the message home: the chatty, romantic youth had overstayed their welcome.

With the home front secured, Rosas then sent armies to the provinces to restore his caudillo allies. Sarmiento and his family hurried to cross the Andes to find refuge in Chile again. For Sarmiento, this began a frantic time of teaching, writing, advocating, and traveling. In 1845, he wrote *Facundo* in installments as he fended off Rosas's extradition demands. Fortunately for Sarmiento, the conservative Chilean government welcomed and protected prestigious Latin American exiles. While not a conservative, Sarmiento appreciated the stability of the Chilean political model. He advocated for public education as the only path to progress for the young South American republics. Somehow, Sarmiento convinced the Chilean government to underwrite a fact-finding mission to Massachusetts, home of the most advanced public education system in the hemisphere, if not the world. From 1845 to 1847, Sarmiento traveled to New England via Brazil, the African coast, and Europe. What an earth-shattering experience that travel must have been! Until that moment, aside from his hometown, the provincial Argentine had only known the austere Chilean capital. Arriving in 1840s Boston, Sarmiento found that the Transcendentalist milieu fit him like a glove. He met Henry Wadsworth Longfellow and the great educators Horace and Mary Mann. The latter took the earnest South American under their wing and

Introduction

became his most enthusiastic and influential supporters. But beyond these strictly intellectual circles, Sarmiento also succumbed to the spectacle of an orderly democratic society. He wrote his observations in a travelogue that some twentieth-century US scholars considered to be on the same level as Alexis de Tocqueville's *Democracy in America*. Sarmiento would have loved to hear that. Sarmiento, like Tocqueville, trusted the self-correcting powers of capitalism and democracy. If only the tyrants had let the citizens do what they knew best!

Back in Argentina, Rosas liked trade, but not of the free kind. For years, he opposed the British attempts to navigate the Paraná and Uruguay and sell their wares upriver. Rosas demanded that all foreign merchant ships unload in Buenos Aires, pay customs, and sell the merchandise to resident port traders. The British navy chafed at Rosas's impertinence and imposed a blockade on the port of Buenos Aires. The blockade lasted from 1845 to 1849 and was at times supported by the French navy. Although Rosas took pride in resisting the European bullies, the blockade mostly hurt consumers in the interior, especially those in the riverine provinces of Entre Ríos, Santa Fe, and Corrientes, whose ports could handle merchant ships and large barges. The independent nation of Paraguay and the southern Brazilian provinces faced the same predicament. Rosas's categorical refusal to allow foreign navigation upriver followed the first Opium War between the British and China. Knowing how the British had responded to the Chinese ban on opium, it was reasonable to expect the same treatment for Buenos Aires. In November 1845, some British vessels blocking the Buenos Aires port broke the chains that closed their access to the Paraná River and, after an artillery exchange with Rosas's land batteries, sailed north to Corrientes, escorting a merchant fleet. Perhaps because the stakes were not as high, however, the British spared Buenos Aires the fate of Shanghai and Canton (Guangzhou). Rosas's stubbornness paid off. In 1849, British negotiators signed a peace treaty that maintained Rosas's conditions on river navigation. After the treaty, trade between Argentina and the United Kingdom resumed, and the wool economy took off. The last three years of the Rosas reign coincided with the arrival of Irish, Scottish, and Basque shepherds and new sheep breeds. Rosas was finally doing what his liberal critics had proposed.

That treaty, however, was his undoing. The caudillo of Entre Ríos, General Justo José de Urquiza, wishing to increase the sheep trade and deal directly with the British, broke the alliance with Rosas. Urquiza was the field commander of the Confederate army and reinforced his troops with units sent by Pedro II of Brazil, the Colorado Party of Uruguay, the

Introduction

Province of Corrientes, and an assortment of Unitarian and liberal exiles, Sarmiento among them. With over thirty thousand men, the largest army ever assembled in the Río de la Plata, Urquiza marched toward Buenos Aires. On February 3, 1852, Urquiza defeated Rosas in a frontal battle in Caseros, a hamlet outside Buenos Aires. The British envoy brokered a plan to let Rosas leave the country and offered him asylum in England. The old rancher, leader of gauchos, the strongman of the Southern Cone, spent the last years of his life in a comfortable cottage near Southampton, tending a 140-acre farm.

The fall of Rosas heralded a new era of peace and prosperity. Or so the victors believed. Alas, it did not take long for disagreements within the diverse anti-Rosas coalition to surface. The returned Unitarian exiles broke with Urquiza over several different issues. The most important was control of the Buenos Aires customs house. On September 11, 1852, Buenos Aires broke with Urquiza and decided not to send delegates to a Constitutional Assembly at the end of the year. The Assembly convened in Santa Fe in January 1853 and worked day and night to complete the constitution in record time. On July 9, 1853, representatives from thirteen Argentine provinces made a solemn oath of loyalty to the Constitution of the Argentine Confederation. Using the indirect system prescribed in the constitution, the provincial representatives elected General Urquiza as the first constitutional president of Argentina. Meanwhile, Buenos Aires declared itself an autonomous state, electing authorities through more or less competitive elections. The Argentine Confederation and the State of Buenos Aires remained in a state of war until 1862, when the army of Buenos Aires, led by General Bartolomé Mitre, another former exiled member of the Generation of 1937, ended the stalemate with a victory in the fields of Pavón. A brutal campaign of retribution followed Mitre's victory against the Federal caudillos of the interior. Only Urquiza remained in control of his province. The repression instigated the caudillo Ángel Vicente Peñaloza, known as Chacho, of La Rioja, to hit back at the national troops in a desperate last-ditch defense of the Federal cause. Sarmiento returned to San Juan as appointed interim (caretaker) governor. His orders were to crush Chacho's rebellion—something he did with gusto.

In 1864, as the Civil War ended in the United States and Mexico resisted the French intervention, a major armed conflict engulfed the Río de la Plata basin. The allied forces of Argentina, Brazil, and Uruguay fought a total war against Paraguay, then led by the strongman Francisco Solano López. It took five years and more than four hundred thousand lives before the allies could defeat the small country. Modern armament, disease, and the belligerents' recklessness made this war the bloodiest in South American history. In Curupayty, on September 22, 1866, the allied commander, the Argentine president Bartolomé Mitre, ordered a frontal attack on two fortified Paraguayan batteries positioned across a waterlogged field. The Paraguayans shelled the unprotected Argentine and Brazilian soldiers for three hours, killing a thousand men and wounding another three thousand. Among the dead was Captain Domingo Fidel Sarmiento, better known as Dominguito, Sarmiento's beloved twenty-year-old son.

Sarmiento received the terrible news in the United States, where he had arrived in May 1865, only weeks after the assassination of Abraham Lincoln, one of his heroes. Sarmiento was in New York, where he was lobbying in favor of the allies and against Paraguay. He found time to research and write a *Life of Lincoln* and participate in the city's vibrant intellectual life. But the death of Dominguito affected him greatly. He was writing notes for a *Life of Dominguito* project and waiting to return to Argentina when he received the news of his nomination as a presidential candidate.

The elections of 1868 were the first elections that did not take place under the shadow of internal strife, although the war was still raging in Paraguay. Four candidates represented different regional and factional interests. One supported Mitre, the incumbent president; another was Urquiza, the caudillo and eternal governor of Entre Ríos. A third was Adolfo Alsina, a popular governor of Buenos Aires Province. Sarmiento was the fourth. Sarmiento's support came from a group of provinces led by Córdoba (ironically, the province that Sarmiento liked to snub for its clericalism). Sarmiento remained in the United States, uninterested in the electoral campaign, perhaps knowing that the governors and their militias would decide the vote anyway. In the electoral college, Sarmiento's name emerged as a consensus candidate, so without campaigning and with no party apparatus, Sarmiento became the president of Argentina.

Compared with the rest of his remarkable career, Sarmiento's six-year presidential term was, arguably, the least exciting period of his life. Argentine history textbooks summarize Sarmiento's presidency with a long paragraph of achievements. Among the highlights, readers learn that Sarmiento established normal schools in each province (and appointed American headmistresses selected by Mary Mann), founded eight hundred new public schools, extended a railroad line to Chivilcoy (a hundred miles) in Buenos Aires Province, founded the Army and Navy academies,

Introduction

inaugurated the Buenos Aires zoo, opened an astronomy observatory in Córdoba, connected Buenos Aires and Córdoba via telegraph, completed the subaquatic telegraphic cable to Montevideo, founded the state-owned Mortgage Bank, and signed the country's Civil Code into law. This scattershot list of policy accomplishments can perhaps be visualized as grading the site for a large building: one can foresee that the structure will be significant, but its shape is barely recognizable.

Sarmiento was an isolated president who lacked loyal partisans and an electoral machine. Cartoonists portrayed him as a pompous statesman, convinced of his importance but detached from reality. He could not do much to increase the country's population (1.8 million people according to the national census he commissioned), eliminate the physical isolation of the provinces, or eradicate the autonomous Indigenous nations in Chaco and Patagonia, as he wished. Illiteracy continued to affect 70 percent of the adult population. Sanitation and health services were so poor that when yellow fever hit Buenos Aires in 1871, it killed more than twelve thousand people, or 8 percent of the population. That calamity took place under Sarmiento's watch.

One of Sarmiento's obsessions that did come to fruition during his government was ending the caudillo rebellions. As mentioned before, Sarmiento began this task as interim governor of San Juan in 1863. Ángel Vicente "Chacho" Peñaloza, a veteran of Quiroga's army and leader of La Rioja's llanos, had led the gauchos against the national government. Chacho attempted to invade San Juan. Troops under Sarmiento's command then rounded up the rebels and killed Chacho, even though he had already surrendered. Sarmiento approved the illegal execution and justified it in letters that stained his reputation as a humanist.

During the war of Paraguay, the Argentine army's heavy-handed recruiting tactics prompted another gaucho rebellion in the interior. Sarmiento was in the United States, mourning his son Dominguito when news of this new caudillo rebellion reached him. On December 10, 1866, Felipe Varela, the last caudillo from La Rioja and a somewhat more enlightened one, issued a manifesto against President Mitre's authoritarianism and mishandling of the Paraguay war. During the austral summer of 1867, Varela and his allies took control of the interior provinces. In April, though, the tide turned against the rebels. By the end of autumn (in June), the interior was back in the hands of the national government, but Varela and a small band of gaucho guerrillas continued resisting, staging attacks from their Andean hideouts, where they disappeared as quickly as they had come. Just after Sarmiento's inauguration in December 1868,

Introduction

Varela struck again. That was the last time, as forces loyal to the national army cut off his escape route.

Sarmiento still had one final caudillo stand to crush. In 1870, in Entre Ríos, the second-line caudillo Ricardo López Jordán rebelled and killed Governor Justo José de Urquiza, the man who had defeated Rosas in 1853. Sarmiento, who had established friendly relations with his old adversary, took Urquiza's assassination as a personal offense. López Jordán's cause was popular in the countryside: he recruited up to eight thousand soldiers in Entre Ríos and Corrientes. These were mainly gaucho cavalrymen armed with bamboo spears and sabers. Only a tiny number were foot soldiers, and they were armed with flintlock rifles. Sarmiento sent three battalions armed with breechloader carbines, Gatling guns, and Krupp cannons. López Jordán's gauchos avoided a pitched battle and used their mobility and knowledge of the terrain to strike, withdraw, and attack again. Still, their numbers dwindled in each encounter. After three years of heroic resistance, López Jordán escaped to Uruguay. Then, at the end of 1876, he returned to Entre Ríos with a small group. When government forces finally defeated and captured López Jordán, the rebellion ended and with it, the age of the caudillos in Argentine history.

The battle scenes of Entre Ríos were a worldwide phenomenon in the second half of the nineteenth century: uniformed soldiers training their rapid-fire guns against hopeless cavalry charges and antique-sword-wielding warriors. These lopsided battles were the precursor of agrarian capitalism. Rhapsodies eulogized the fallen heroes sacrificed to the deity of Progress while swarms of surveyors, notaries, auctioneers, land speculators, and profit-seeking tenants turned the peasant communities and the open range into commercial real estate. After López Jordán's gauchos, it was the turn of the Indigenous people of Patagonia and Chaco to get the Remington treatment. During Sarmiento's administration, the national army had advanced slowly but steadily against the Mapuche confederation that controlled the western half of Buenos Aires Province, the southern quarters of Córdoba, San Luis, and Mendoza, and the future territories of Neuquén, La Pampa, and Río Negro. President Nicolás Avellaneda, who succeeded Sarmiento in 1874, gave General Julio Roca the authority to annihilate the Mapuche confederation and take over their vast domain. Roca began his campaign at the end of 1878. By early 1880, hundreds of thousands of Mapuche people were dead or had been subjected to forced labor or reduced to minor reservations in the Patagonian steppe. The Chaco Indigenous nations came next. By 1888, the Argentine map looked approximately like its current version.

Introduction

During the years that followed Sarmiento's presidency, Argentina experienced rapid territorial, economic, and demographic growth. European immigrants began arriving in steady numbers. By 1890, half a million Italians, two hundred thousand Spaniards, one hundred thousand French (mostly Basques), and one hundred thousand other migrants of diverse European nationalities had arrived at the port of Buenos Aires. Half of them remained as permanent residents. Immigration continued to grow until the 1930s, with a short hiatus during the First World War. Sarmiento lived long enough to observe the immigration process taking on a life of its own. The same can be said for the policies that Sarmiento advocated for and helped shape. These included opening the country to foreign capital, stimulating investment in railroads, consigning national lands for agricultural colonies, consolidating the monopoly of violence in the national state institutions, and extricating the city of Buenos Aires from the homonymous province (thus shrinking Buenos Aires's elite power). It was, however, the two-term president General Julio A. Roca (1880–1886, 1898–1904), the victor of the campaign against the Mapuche, who took credit for Argentina's spectacular results in all those policy areas.

Sarmiento retired from public office in 1879, but not from public life. He continued working on his dearest brainchild: the Argentine public education system. In 1882, he led the First Pedagogical Congress in Buenos Aires. By recommendation of this meeting, the Argentine Congress made elementary education compulsory, accessible, and secular. Meanwhile, Sarmiento continued writing, which, in hindsight, may not have been the most fabulous idea. His last book, *Conflicts and Harmony among Races in the Americas*, published in 1883, is a rambling repetition of the racist clichés taught as a social science in American and British universities, applied to individualized ethnic groups in Latin America. In this hastily written text, Sarmiento bemoaned that Latin Americans were racially incapable of achieving progress. They were not Anglo-Saxons, and that was a fact that even mass immigration would not change. *Conflicts and Harmony* is a far cry from the stylistic brilliance of *Facundo*, and it is evidence that Sarmiento had moved toward a biological explanation of the civilization/barbarism dichotomy. However, despite the book's racist pessimism, Sarmiento kept to his old faith in the progressive effects of public education, even among the populations he declared racially unfit. Furthermore, Sarmiento saw that Latin America's only chance to withstand the looming US hegemony was to educate the nonwhite masses. That point resonated with many contemporary Latin American

Introduction

intellectuals, who were equally concerned about the nonwhiteness of their nations and the influence of the United States.

Sarmiento, Author of a Nation is the title of a 1994 collection of essays about our author. The bombastic title, however, does not reflect either the critical contributions to this volume or even reality. Was Argentina ever the crystallization of Sarmiento's dreams? Perhaps, on the eve of the Depression, when European immigrants and their children outnumbered nonwhite Argentines, public school access had become near-universal, and the GDP per capita matched those of Canada and Australia, Argentina looked like what Sarmiento had envisioned. But fast forward two decades, and the liberal illusion disappears. Had Sarmiento traveled in time to 1950s Buenos Aires, he would have probably loved the jaunty capital (and the many sculptures dedicated to his likeness). But he would not have recognized the elite intellectuals who invoked his name but had shed nineteenth-century liberal secularism in order to adopt the "myth of the Catholic nation," a reactionary ideology with apparent connections to the contemporary French and Spanish far-right. And worse, Sarmiento would have been appalled by the irrational devotion that the common folk, educated in the public schools he had helped create, showered on Juan and Eva Perón, much as their gaucho ancestors had professed admiration for Rosas and Quiroga. Time-traveling Sarmiento would not have claimed his authorship of this Argentina.

And yet, though Sarmiento may not have authored Argentina, it is undoubtedly the case that the country and the larger-than-life writer followed entwined paths. Argentina and Sarmiento were born and—to follow up the metaphor—reached adulthood simultaneously. If Sarmiento's writings, along with those of his friends and rivals of the Generation of 1837, shaped the legal scaffolding of the nation, everything that Sarmiento was resulted from growing up in the uncertain though intellectually stimulating times of nation-state formation. Foremost, Sarmiento's profile as a public intellectual rested on his unwavering opposition to caudillo rule. This tension resulted from his birth in the formerly peaceful, uneventful San Juan Valley. The arid basin that rings the valley from east and south, with its fast-riding gauchos and uncouth ranchers, always loomed over the sedentary valley dwellers. The civil wars opened the floodgates, and San Juan became the target of raiding bands of gauchos with political opinions and little taste for social deference. For Sarmiento, Federalism spelled caudillo rule, which meant the loss of the valley's peace and his family's means of living. Uprooted, he then traveled the world, accentuating, with readings and observations, his belief in the epic struggle of civilization

Introduction

against barbarism. He spent most of his life fighting the caudillos and won the last battle in Entre Ríos. Building civilization through public education proved more complicated. It required years of investment and patient training of human resources, which the following generations would have to complete. Argentina was still a work in progress when Sarmiento died.

In the last years of his life, Sarmiento developed an affection for the city of Asunción, in Paraguay. In this country, his son had fallen in battle, and he had collaborated in its destruction, but he had friends in the postwar liberal elite. Asunción's mild winters also suited the rapidly aging Sarmiento well. At the onset of the austral winter of 1888, he traveled to Asunción, followed by his surviving family and a baggage train of books and papers. He died of a heart attack on September 11 of that year. After his death, the Buenos Aires newspapers published a lithograph based on a postmortem picture arranged by his doctor and family. Sarmiento appears to be relaxing on a reclining chair, exhausted after a long day of hard work; on his right side, piling up on a desk, a mountain of papers awaits his attention.

FURTHER READINGS

Brown, Jonathan. *A Brief History of Argentina.* New York: Facts on File Inc., 2011.

Criscenti, Joseph T. *Sarmiento and His Argentina.* Boulder, CO: L. Rienner Publishers, 1993.

De la Fuente, Ariel. *Children of Facundo: Caudillo and Gaucho Insurgency during the Argentine State-Formation Process (La Rioja, 1853–1870).* Durham, NC: Duke University Press, 2000.

Halperín Donghi, Tulio et al. *Sarmiento, Author of a Nation.* Berkeley: University of California Press, 1994.

Hooker, Juliet. *Theorizing Race in the Americas: Douglass, Sarmiento, Du Bois and Vasconcelos,* 67–110. Oxford: Oxford University Press, 2019.

Katra, William H. *The Argentine Generation of 1837: Echeverría, Alberdi, Sarmiento, Mitre.* Madison, NJ: Fairleigh Dickinson University Press, 1996.

Scobie, James R. *Buenos Aires: Plaza to Suburb, 1870–1910.* New York: Oxford University Press, 1974.

Sorensen, Diana. *Facundo and the Construction of Argentine Culture.* Austin: University of Texas Press, 1996.

CHRONOLOGY

27 Nov 1788   Facundo Quiroga is born in San Antonio, La Rioja

25 May 1810   "May Revolution": Buenos Aires breaks away from Spain

11 Feb 1811   Domingo Faustino Sarmiento is born in San Juan

9 July 1816   Declaration of Independence of the United Provinces of Río de la Plata

1817   General San Martín's liberation campaign in Chile

1819   Constitution of the United Provinces

1820   Battle of Cepeda: dissolution of the United Provinces. Each province reassumes sovereignty

March 1823   Facundo Quiroga elected governor of La Rioja

Dec 1824   Reunification of the United Provinces; the National Congress is under control of the Unitarian party

1825   Bernardino Rivadavia appointed President of the Republic. Quiroga leads the Federal opposition in the interior

1825   Argentina-Brazil War begins

1826   The National Congress passes a Unitarian constitution; the provinces controlled by Quiroga reject the constitution

1828   Peace with Brazil; independence of Uruguay

1828   Dissolution of the national government

1828   Civil war breaks out between the Unitarian and Federal parties

1829   Federal caudillo Juan Manuel de Rosas becomes governor of Buenos Aires

1831   Sarmiento goes into first exile in Chile

Oct 1835   Assassination of Facundo Quiroga in Córdoba

1837   Sarmiento is back in San Juan; founds a newspaper and a school

1838   Sarmiento goes into exile in Chile for a second time

1845   In Chile, Sarmiento publishes *Facundo: Civilization and Barbarism*

1852   Battle of Caseros; a coalition army led by Federal general Justo Urquiza defeats Rosas

Chronology

1853 Constitution of the Argentine Confederation; Buenos Aires secedes from the confederation

1853 War between the state of Buenos Aires and the Argentine Confederation begins; Sarmiento appointed to several offices in the state of Buenos Aires

1862 End of Buenos Aires secession; Argentina changes its name from Confederation to Republic. Bartolomé Mitre (Nationalist party) becomes president

1863 Sarmiento serving as interim governor of San Juan. Rebellion of Chacho Peñaloza

1864 Paraguayan war begins

1865 Sarmiento begins serving as Argentine ambassador to the United States

1866 Battle of Curupayty, Paraguay; Domingo F. Sarmiento, Jr.—Dominguito—dies in action

1868–1874 Sarmiento: President of Argentina

1874–1880 President Nicolás Avellaneda (Partido Autonomista Nacional)

1880 Conquest of Southern Pampas and Patagonia. Extermination of Indigenous nations

1880 Buenos Aires becomes a federal district and official capital of Argentina

1880–1884 President Julio A. Roca (Partido Autonomista Nacional)

1882 National Pedagogical Congress

11 Sept 1888 Death of Sarmiento

Map of Latin America

Latin America today. Note that the west coast of South America is almost in line with the east coast of North America.

Map of Argentina

Argentina today, with provinces and major geographic regions and features. In Sarmiento's time, cities like Córdoba and the more densely populated port city of Buenos Aires contrasted with vast expanses of unpopulated territory, which left their mark on Sarmiento's thinking and writing.

1. *Facundo*: The Shaping of a Paradigm

Sarmiento's *Facundo* is one of the top two or three most influential essays ever written about Latin America. While the life of Facundo Quiroga served as the pretext for the essay and inspired the title, the main focus was on the clash between civilization and barbarism, which the subtitle of the book makes clear. For Sarmiento, this dichotomy pitted things urban and European against things rural and native to Latin America. Things urban and European were civilized and to be encouraged. Things rural and native were barbarous and to be eliminated. Sarmiento did not invent the dichotomy. To the contrary, it loomed over nineteenth-century Latin America as an interpretive paradigm even before he wrote. But *Facundo* was to become the primary statement of this dichotomy and Sarmiento its best-known exponent. It is no exaggeration to say that a basic knowledge of Latin American literature and history *requires* some exposure to Sarmiento's *Facundo*.

Here readers will find the core of *Facundo*, including colorful descriptions of gaucho "types" and a fast-paced account of the caudillo leader Facundo Quiroga's early years. In addition to these passages we also find Sarmiento's engaging assessment of daily activities at *pulperías* (dry-goods stores that doubled as taverns) and their impact on Argentine social life.

❊ ❊ ❊

FACUNDO

On ne tue point les idées.
—Fortoul[1]

At the end of the year 1840, I was leaving my country, exiled for pity's sake. Also full of cuts and bruises, inflicted the day before by my tormentors, soldiers and bloodthirsty partisans of the dictator Rosas. Passing the Zonda hot springs on my way, underneath a picture of our national coat of arms that I had drawn, in happier days, on the wall of one of the bathhouses, I scrawled this quotation of Fortoul with a bit of charred wood on the white-plastered wall. "You can slit a throat," as one of my countrymen might say, "but you can't kill an idea."

Informed of my heinous act, the government sent armed men to decipher my strange hieroglyphics, which were rumored to contain the most ignoble sort of threats and insults. Someone translated my French, and the ruffians scratched their heads. "Can't kill an idea. What does he mean by that?"

It meant simply that I was coming here, to Chile, where the light of Liberty still shone, promising to use Chilean newspapers to shine the light of liberty across the Andes to my homeland. Have I kept my promise?

Speak, you who have known me in Santiago.

Introduction[2]

Ghost of Facundo, arise from the grave! I command you!

Cast aside the bloodstained earth that covers your remains, and arise to explain the fratricidal conflicts that have put our noble people perpetually at each other's throats since our independence from Spain. What is your evil secret? I inquire because you, yes you, instigated that fratricide, and ten years after your assassination at Barranca Bermejo, many people in Argentina still say: "No, no, he isn't dead! Facundo lives!"

---

1. "You cannot kill an idea." Hippolyte Fortoul, a French writer and politician. For Sarmiento and other nineteenth-century writers and statespeople, quoting French authors and sources in French was meant to demonstrate erudition, refinement, and global intellectual stature.
2. This translation is a condensation of the chapter-length introduction to the 1845 edition, *Obras*, vol. 7, pp. 5–14.

1. Facundo: The Shaping of a Paradigm

And it's true. You live in the stories told by the common people and in the political conflicts at the center of those stories. You live on, most importantly, in the dictator Juan Manuel de Rosas himself. Your soul apparently transmigrated, upon your assassination, into the body of your political heir and complement, the tyrant Rosas. The tyrant Rosas, one could say, is the fulfillment and culmination of your oeuvre. What was instinct, inspiration, and improvisation in you became, in Rosas, system, policy, and premeditation. You were a true barbarian, an unpretentious rustic; Rosas is the favorite son of our cosmopolitan capital city, who nonetheless successfully presents himself as the embodiment of our rural traditions. The audacious provincial has been replaced by a cold and calculating Machiavelli. Facundo's awful promise is fulfilled in the tyrant Rosas.

The sycophants of the tyrant proclaim his unrivaled greatness, and sadly, they are quite correct. The villainy of Rosas is unrivaled in the entire world. All his misdeeds are superlatives. He has inspired thousands to harness themselves to his war chariot and heave it onward over a pavement of corpses. He has inspired thousands more to resist him by any means imaginable during fifteen years of relentless turmoil. They cannot, must not, give up the struggle, for Rosas stands squarely athwart the path to political organization of the Argentine Republic.

Rosas is the Argentine Sphinx, half woman and half tiger, and like the original, he demands that passersby solve his riddle. What was the secret of Facundo's power? Whosoever solves this riddle, and is able to redirect the popular influence exercised by Facundo in life, holds the key to our political salvation! Only after we have rid ourselves of Facundo's ghost will the Argentine Republic be able to assume its proper place of honor among the nations of the New World.

Today, the Argentine Republic is the part of Spanish America most observed by European nations. They are seemingly fascinated by the whirling vortex of our internal affairs. England has more than once involved itself in our struggles, and France, as well, was recently at the point of being drawn into them. European observers uniformly fail to understand Argentina, however. South America, and particularly Argentina, has not yet found its Tocqueville, not yet hosted the visit of a trained outsider possessing the requisite curiosity, theoretical understanding, and information-gathering tools to make sense of our mysteries. Without such an author to explain us, the stubborn conflicts that have torn at the Argentine Republic for years remain an enigma in the eyes of the civilized world.

1. Facundo: *The Shaping of a Paradigm*

Due consideration has not been given to the formative role of the natural environment, nor to the traditions and habits left to us by our Spanish colonizers, nor to the Indigenous influences that remain powerful, nor to the more recently introduced influences of progressive European civilization, nor even to the more-than-democratic tendencies instilled in us by our wars for independence. A proper study of post-independence Argentina by competent European observers would have revealed an astounding new political world, a knock-down, drag-out contest pitting the cities against the wilderness, pitting the most recent progress of the human spirit against the most primitive sort of backwardness—a contest, in sum, between civilization and barbarism.

Such a study would have explained much more than events in the Argentine Republic. An appreciation of the Spanish legacy in America clarifies the root of anti-modern tendencies elsewhere in the continent, in Paraguay, for example, where the theological dictator Doctor Francia rivals our militaristic dictator Rosas in authoritarian closed-mindedness. All across South America, nativist parties, claiming to represent our authentic "American" culture but actually representing the cultural heritage of Spain, oppose "European" influence when it comes from enlightened countries like England or France.

Relegated to exile in Chile, what can one do to oppose this travesty? How can one support the intrepid Argentines who refuse to give up their dreams of national betterment? Only by lending them a voice denied to them by the tyrant's repression of the press in Argentina. Let my voice tell the untold story, then, not of the tyrant Rosas, whose story is unfortunately not yet at an end, but, rather, the story of Juan Facundo Quiroga, the tyrant's brutish colleague and rival. To solve the riddle of Argentina's long struggle to build a nation-state, we must study the constituent elements of that struggle, including its antecedents and the landscape upon which it has played out, as well as the customs and traditions of its inhabitants. Facundo's story exemplifies the barbarism that clashes today with civilization in countries throughout Spanish America.

Now that Facundo has been dead ten years, the time has come to write his biography. This undertaking has been possible for me to attempt because, although lacking in the expertise of a Tocqueville, I do possess local knowledge. Facundo and I were born in the same region of Argentina, in the eastern foothills of the Andes. Thus, I have been able to draw on personal memories of him, and I have also tapped the memories of many eyewitnesses, countrymen of mine who knew Facundo at all stages of his career, from the time of his youth. Much information has arrived in

1. Facundo: The Shaping of a Paradigm

my hands by post, and more arrives daily. I beg anyone who notices an inaccuracy in my account to bring it immediately to my attention. Even the smallest detail must be accurate, because our subject is much bigger than the life of one man. Instead, it is the cultural legacy of a country, and to some degree, of an entire continent.

Chapter 1[3]
Physical Geography and Its Impact on the Argentine Republic

The South American continent comes to a point at its southern extremity, below the Strait of Magellan. To the west, only a short distance from the Pacific Ocean and parallel to the coast, runs the high ridge of the Chilean Andes. All the territory to the east of the Andes, focused on the Río de la Plata estuary, with Paraguay and Bolivia and Brazil to the north, is Argentina. Blood is still being spilled to determine whether it shall be a unified republic or a confederation.

The immense majority of the country is not populated by farmers. There are fully navigable rivers where no sort of civilized craft has ever ventured. The first problem which afflicts the Argentine Republic is its vast expanse. The desert surrounds it.[4] Solitude and wilderness without human habitation isolate its provinces from one another. There is immensity everywhere. Immense plains, woods, and rivers, the horizon always uncertain, always blended with the earth among varicolored clouds and tenuous vapors which prevent us from determining the distant point at which the world ends and the sky begins. Herds of horses and cattle graze extensively.

Among the forests to the south and the north, savages prowl through the undergrowth, awaiting moonlit nights, to then go out upon the plain and, like a pack of hyenas, ravage defenseless herds and settlements. Long trains of carts, each drawn by six oxen and supported by two enormous wheels, crisscross the pampas, scanning the horizon constantly, guarding against an unprovoked surprise attack. They camp in a defensible position to pass the night. Perhaps some noise gets their attention as they sit around the campfire eating. Sudden silence, all eyes on the horizon. If

---

3. Translated from the Biblioteca Ayacucho edition of *Facundo*, 1977.
4. Sarmiento is not using the term "desert" literally, but rather to refer to vast expanses with few or no inhabitants, urban infrastructure, or institutions, and thus lacking in civilization.

1. Facundo: The Shaping of a Paradigm

they hear and see nothing further, they still check the ears of the horses grazing nearby. Are the animals' ears motionless and relaxed? If so, the meal and the conversation continue uninterrupted. And of course, there are pumas and poisonous snakes to deal with, as well.

The permanent and habitual insecurity of life in the countryside of Argentina has, to my thinking, left a palpable mark on the Argentine character. There is a stoic resignation toward violent death as a never-quite-unexpected accompaniment of life, a way to die like any other. This general attitude perhaps explains, at least in part, the unexpressive indifference with which rural Argentine males abruptly kill other men or unexpectedly encounter their own violent death. Nor does one find any particular, lingering trauma in the survivors of such shocking episodes.

The inhabited parts of Argentina can be divided into three zones, each with a different sort of environment. To the north, merging into the tropical region of the Great Chaco, extends a dense, unbroken canopy of low forest. One would call it "unbelievably immense," if immensity were not so common in the landscapes of the Americas. Next, descending toward the south, one encounters a transitional zone in which forest and grasslands contend for dominance. Here the forest fragments and degenerates occasionally into thorny brush, but returns in strength to line the riverbanks until, finally, it gives way altogether to the smooth, flat, downy surface of the pampa, which stretches away toward the southern horizon as a featureless, and apparently limitless, plain. The pampa gives the appearance of a terrestrial sea, vast spaces still awaiting the appearance of any sort of agriculture.

A notable trait of this land is the agglomeration of navigable rivers. Many great rivers converge toward the Río de la Plata estuary, which combines their flow to deliver its stupendous aquatic tribute to the Atlantic Ocean. But these immense canals excavated by Nature's solicitous hand have left no mark on the custom of the Argentine people. An Argentine countryman considers himself imprisoned in the narrow confines of a boat. When a great river cuts off his passage, he calmly undresses, prepares his horse, and guides it swimming to an islet made out from afar. There the horse and rider rest before attempting the next leg of the crossing, and from islet to islet the crossing is finished at last. Thus, the Argentine countryman disdains to navigate these river roads, the greatest favor that Providence has supplied to the country, seeing them only as an obstacle to his movements. Thus, the God-given facility of river navigation (and, by extension, canal transportation), as potentially empowering as the navigation of the Nile or the Rhine or the Mississippi, is utterly disregarded

1. Facundo: The Shaping of a Paradigm

by those dwelling along the stupendous currents of the Bermejo, the Pilcomayo, the Paraná, the Paraguay, and the Uruguay Rivers. A pitiful few riverboats crewed by Italians ascend the Paraná and the Uruguay Rivers for a short distance, but further north and west, all fluvial navigation vanishes. Our Spanish colonizers simply did not possess the navigational instincts so highly developed among northern Europeans. The potentially vivifying arteries of our national life, the rivers that could enrich the provinces of Santa Fe, Entre Ríos, Corrientes, Córdoba, Salta, Tucumán, and Jujuy beyond the wildest dreams of their current inhabitants, require a new and different sort of spirit to make them functional.

At present, all the benefits of maritime access to our national market go to the two principal Río de la Plata ports, Montevideo and Buenos Aires, which stand respectively on the northern and southern banks of the great muddy estuary where all our great rivers converge to enter the Atlantic Ocean. Its enviable geographic location seems destined to make the city of Buenos Aires, in particular, a gigantic trade emporium, easily among the most important of the Americas. In fact, with a beneficent climate and a vast hinterland under its commercial control, monopolizing virtually all Argentina's overseas trade and contact with Europe, Buenos Aires would already have achieved its destiny, were it not for the baneful influence of the thirteen interior provinces that depend on it commercially and dominate it culturally. Buenos Aires denies to its hinterland all the industrial and demographic advantages conferred by direct contact with the overseas centers of world civilization. Buoyed up by its trade monopoly, Buenos Aires has been stupidly deaf to the interior provinces' clamor for a share of its privileged access to the world. The interior provinces, ignored by the great port and thereby deprived of access to civilization, have revenged themselves by drowning the city of Buenos Aires in their own barbaric spirit, embodied today in the tyrant Rosas.

The blame does not lie so much with the city of Buenos Aires. Its greatness has accrued automatically from its geographic advantages. The fault lies with Providence itself, that made such an unequal distribution of those advantages. But of course, it avails us of nothing to rage against Providence. Let us instead accept what we cannot change and rectify the ignorant policies that have impeded a more generous distribution of the benefits that flow therefrom. The current policies of Buenos Aires do nothing to promote the economic and cultural development of the interior provinces. Instead of spreading light and wealth, Buenos Aires subjugates and humiliates its hinterland. Until now, the benefits of progress and civilization have accumulated only in the city of Buenos

1. Facundo: The Shaping of a Paradigm

Aires. Moreover, far from being a good conductor, the cultural milieu of the surrounding pampa countryside is actually hostile to progress and actively impedes the diffusion of European civilization to Argentina's provincial capitals. All this must change, of course, but for now, it's a stark reality. The current tyranny of Rosas contrasts grievously with the dream we "unitarians" dreamt, but in truth the lay of the land in Argentina has always lent itself to centralized control—that of Buenos Aires, the principal port.

Another reality of this place, one that defines and unifies it, from north to south and east to west, from the Andes to the Atlantic, is its constant, uniform flatness. Whether clothed in tall, luxuriant tropical forest; in scrubby, thorny, arid-land vegetation; or only lightly, by the smoothness of pampas grasses—the landscapes of Argentina are ubiquitously flat. The general flatness completely overwhelms minor challenges such as the so-called mountains of Córdoba or San Luis and a few stray Andean ridges in the northwest. When, one day, these fertile lands gain the right population under the right social conditions, the flatness of the Argentine Republic will contribute to our national unity, for it is well known that, by limiting transportation, mountains breed isolation, and isolation generates cultural distinctions and facilitates lingering primitive holdouts. The lay of the land in North America makes the United States a natural federation. A string of separate colonies along the Atlantic coast, along with the vast interior navigation systems represented by the Mississippi and Saint Lawrence Rivers, provided rulers no single choke point by which to control access to the Atlantic economy. The Argentine Republic, by contrast, is truly "one and indivisible."

Thus, the limitless, thinly populated plains that stretch more than seven hundred leagues from Buenos Aires to Salta and Mendoza constitute the most notable interior feature of the Argentine Republic. There is something almost Oriental about these solitudes. The gauchos are reminiscent of bedouins, and one almost expects to see, on occasion, a line of camels plodding toward Baghdad. The pampa analog are caravans of enormous two-wheeled oxcarts that roll freely without encountering the least obstacle, without needing the hand of man to clear the way of trees or thickets. No more than the efforts of the individual and the effects of the natural environment are needed to open avenues of communication. Society can do little to improve them.

The leader of one of these caravans needs an iron will, a character bold to the point of recklessness, to defend and dominate his subordinates amid the solitude. At the least sign of insolence, he raises his mighty

1. Facundo: *The Shaping of a Paradigm*

iron-handed lash and dishes out wounds and contusions. If resistance continues, rather than his pistols, which he seldom deigns to draw, he applies his long knife. He leaps from his horse, blade in hand, and quickly reestablishes his authority by the superior skill with which he wields the countryman's common weapon. Thus, the material conditions of Argentine life establish the primacy of brute force, the superiority of the strongest, the authority without limits or responsibility of those who give the orders. On these long journeys, the common people of Argentina acquire the habits of life outside of society, hardened by privations, struggling individually with nature, depending only on their personal capacity and wit against the dangers that surround them continually.

The population that dwells in these extensive regions is composed largely of two different races, Spanish and Indian, that mix together to form an array of intermediate shades. Variations run across the spectrum. In parts of Córdoba and San Luis live some country people of purely Spanish extraction. There one encounters shepherd girls entirely as white and rosy-cheeked as the European version. In Santiago del Estero, on the other hand, the bulk of the rural population speaks Quechua, an unmistakable mark of Indigenous origin. In Corrientes, people speak an amusing blend of Spanish and Guaraní. A third race, of African descent, has almost disappeared except in the province of Buenos Aires, leaving behind its own intermediate shades of mixture with Spanish and Indian.

With some exceptions, these three races have fused in a rural population distinguished by its love of idleness and lack of industry. This unfortunate situation seems to have resulted mostly from the Spanish colonizers' social incorporation of native races that have shown themselves incapable of hard, sustained labor even when compelled by force. It was that incapacity, precisely, which led to the importation of African slaves, with fatal consequences for our society. Nor has the Spanish race proved much more industrious than the native or African races when abandoned to its instincts amid the wilderness of America. Only education and the incentive of social betterment can hope to improve the national population.

It is pathetic and shameful to compare rural settlements of native Argentines in the Province of Buenos Aires with the settlements of German or Scottish immigrants. In the latter, the houses are painted, their front yards always neat and planted with flowers and shrubbery. The furniture is simple but adequate. The tableware is of copper or tin, but brightly polished. The inhabitants are in constant motion, milking cows to make cheese and butter, from which some families have managed

1. Facundo: The Shaping of a Paradigm

to amass fortunes large enough to enable them to move to the city and enjoy the comforts of urban life. In the rural homes of native Argentines, however, the situation is unhappily reversed. Unkempt, ragged children scurry in packs there, like dogs, filth and poverty everywhere. Men lie around on the ground, in the most complete inactivity. A small table and a hide-covered box or two may be the only furniture in each miserable hut, notable for its general appearance of barbarism and carelessness.

Amid the limitless spaces that we have described stand fourteen cities, scattered here and there, the provincial capitals. In rough geographical order, then, Buenos Aires, Santa Fe, Entre Ríos, and Corrientes are eastern cities, located on the banks of the Paraná River. Far to the west, located along the foothills of the Andes, stand six more provincial capitals: Mendoza, San Juan, La Rioja, Catamarca, Salta, and Jujuy. And finally, near the center of the country, are Santiago, San Luis, and Córdoba. What really interests us, however, is not location but way of life. A rural population's way of life, its primary economic activity, defines its character and spirit. And all the provincial cities of Argentina, with the exception of San Juan and Mendoza with their vineyards, depend almost exclusively on the pastoral economy. Their products are meat, wool, and leather. Tucumán sugar adds a bit more to the picture, as does the modern array of trades in bustling Buenos Aires. As for rural Buenos Aires Province, however, the crushing dominance of livestock raising pertains in full force.

Argentine cities have the regular layout of almost all Spanish cities in America. Their streets intersect at right angles and their habitations are widely spaced, excepting only the case of Córdoba, which is denser and made more European-looking by the domes and bell towers of its numerous churches. Cities are the locus of Argentine, Spanish, European civilization. In cities, one finds commerce and industry, justice and education, government and laws, notions of progress, everything, in sum, that characterizes a people of culture and refinement. The man of our cities wears European clothing and leads a civilized life such as that of civilized men anywhere else. In the provincial capitals one finds refined tastes and an awareness of contemporary European styles, but these miniature replicas of civilization are surrounded and engulfed by the endless pampa. The provincial capital is frequently the only urban center in the province.

When one sets foot outside the provincial capitals, the look of everything changes. The man of the countryside wears different clothing and leads a totally different life. Far from desiring to imitate the urban man,

1. Facundo: The Shaping of a Paradigm

the country man rejects European luxuries and scorns refined manners and clothing. Anyone who dares show himself in the country wearing a tailcoat, for example, or mounting an English saddle, would attract aggressive mockery, or worse, from the people of the countryside. In the countryside, society lapses into feudalism or disappears completely. Governance becomes impossible because the police cannot exercise their function and the courts have no way to extend their control over criminals. Domestic life loses its moral compass as curates abandon their solitary chapels, and religion lapses. Civilization itself founders, and barbarism becomes the normal state of affairs.

Society is relatively absent in the Argentine countryside. First, this is because we are herders, and pastoral activities are always less social than farming. Still, the absence of social life in rural Argentina is extreme. The herders of Arabia are nomads, but they live in societies held together by ancient traditions and religious convictions, under the leadership of tribal elders. Their cultural development is retarded by their nomadism, but at least they live in society. The gauchos of Argentina lack even that. Their small family groups live in solitude, scattered across the infinite pampa at distances that eliminate all human contact, in simple dwellings separated from one another by many miles. Unlike the roving Arab band, our gauchos can own private property, but to what end? Why construct a luxurious abode which no visitors will ever arrive to admire? Without social stimulus, the strictures of civilized behavior gradually relax and barbarism takes over. The result is a kind of feudalism. No sort of governance is possible over these isolated families who lack all the advantages of European villagers. Perhaps this organization resembles that of the early Slavic peoples, but it contrasts with the Roman municipality, in which the entire population inhabited the village and went out daily to farm the fields. The social organization of the ancient Romans produced modern civilization. All we can boast in Argentina are men with the style and outlook of feudal barons, whose principal public function is to periodically terrorize defenseless city dwellers. Because our feudal barons do not possess castles or mountain strongholds, however, they lack staying power. No feudal action can survive an immediate reaction. The political projects of the pampa ebb and flow like the tides, creating momentary disturbances but never any cumulative transformation.

In one thing only does the citizen of rural Argentina match the classic model. He does not have to work. The citizen of Rome or Sparta had slaves to grow food for him and his family; the gaucho has livestock to do it for him. Left to themselves, the animals seek their own food supply,

1. Facundo: The Shaping of a Paradigm

multiply, and care for their young. The herder need only watch over them and, occasionally, separate one of them to sacrifice for his meal. But our gauchos lack the outlet that the ancient Romans and Greeks directed to the forum, the public square, the affairs of state. There are no gatherings of cattle herders to resolve collective problems, because there is no collective. Argentine pastoral society has reached a developmental dead end. It cannot move to a higher level because, strictly speaking, there is no society there. And without public matters, in Latin *res publica*, there can be no "republic."

The bonds of religion dissolve, in this situation, along with other social bonds. The local curate, if there still is one, loses his moral compass in the social vacuum and, often enough, emerges as a renegade leader. Now family takes over religious life as well, uniting patriarchal and priestly functions in an almost biblical manner. I recall my stay in the hills of San Luis, in 1838, at the house of an old rancher whose two favorite activities were praying and gambling. The local curate had disappeared long since, but the rancher had built a chapel on his ranch where he publicly prayed the rosary in the afternoon. It was like a scene from the Old Testament or, possibly, a Homeric epic—the sun bending low to the horizon, the bleating sheep returning to their nightly enclosure, the blue-eyed patriarch of broad forehead and wispy beard intoning the ancient formulas as a knot of women responded in chorus. Several half-grown boys stood uneasily around the chapel door, holding the reins of half-tamed horses and adding little volume to the responses. The old man's prayer concluded with fervent words, beseeching rain for the pastures, fecundity for the lowing beasts, safety for the travelers of windswept roads, and peace for the Republic. I have never witnessed a purer or more natural expression of religious sentiment. I felt that I could be in the presence of Abraham.

But purity and fervor are not enough to maintain a healthy religious life. However fervent, religion in the Argentine countryside has been reduced to its lowest denominator. Like the Spanish language, Catholicism persists in a corrupt form, undermined by superstitions, devoid of institutional controls. And the inhabitants of our countryside clearly recognize the insufficiency of their religious educations. When priests visit isolated rural areas, they are deluged with requests to baptize children, and sometimes even traveling merchants get such requests.

In the absence of all means of civilization and progress, which can only develop when people are gathered in a numerous society, behold the education of Argentina's rural citizenry. Women take care of the house, prepare the food, shear the sheep, milk the cows, make the cheese, and

1. Facundo: The Shaping of a Paradigm

weave the crude fabric from which the clothing is made. All domestic and household labors, virtually all work of any kind, rests on the shoulders of the woman. At best, the man may plant a bit of corn for his family, but little and rarely, for no kind of bread figures in its daily diet. The children obviously do not attend school. Where would one locate schools in a countryside with a completely dispersed rural population? The children develop their physical strength in play. If male, they begin to practice the use of the lasso on goats and calves, and as soon as they begin to ride horseback, which they do not long after learning to walk, they are off across the countryside. By the time they have become young men, they achieve complete independence and also utter idleness. Their education is at an end, and little remains, besides the Spanish language and a few confused notions of Catholicism, to recall their more distant social origins. At that point, they have become gauchos.

One must see, in order to believe, the indomitable character that emerges from this education, from this struggle of the isolated individual against nature. One must see the grave expressions of the gauchos, framed by beard and tousled hair like that of an Arab, to appreciate the disdain with which they regard the sedentary city dweller, who may have read many books but has no idea how to take down a wild bull, who has not the faintest notion how to catch and mount a mustang when finding himself on foot, alone, on the open pampa, who has never faced a puma's attack by thrusting one poncho-wrapped hand into the mouth of the lunging animal while driving his knife into its heart with the other hand. Their incessant individual struggles against nature have given Argentines of whatever class a prodigious national arrogance that offends the other people of America, who often accuse them of excessive vanity.[5] I do not deny the charge but do not regret its truth. Woe to the nation without faith in itself, for it will never accomplish great things.

The independence of South America gained impetus, no doubt, from the arrogance of these Argentine gauchos who claim never to have met their own match among all the wise and powerful men of the earth. The cultured European is a laughingstock in their eyes because of his exotic clothing and his clumsiness on horseback. Nor is the gauchos' scorn affectionate, but rather, deep and implacable. It is easy to imagine how such qualities have contributed to their effectiveness as soldiers. And if their brute courage and disregard of physical privations were insufficient preparation for war, imagine their habit of slaughter. From a young age,

---

5. The stereotype of "the arrogant Argentine" is still common throughout Latin America.

herders learn to slit the throats, periodically, of the animals that they herd. This necessary, habitual action familiarizes them with the spilling of blood and hardens their hearts against the spasms of the victims.

In sum, the education of Argentine gauchos develops their bodies but not their minds. Triumph over repeated physical challenges makes them proud and energetic. With no formal education at all, and with no perceived need for it, the gaucho lives with heedless satisfaction amid a poverty that he scarcely notices. But if the gaucho is incapable of participation in a well-constituted society, his life is not devoid of attractions. His food and clothing can be gotten without onerous labor, because the gaucho regards working the livestock as his favorite sport. Rural men eagerly await roundup and branding time, an intense collective activity analogous to the harvest and processing of grapes at a large vineyard. Gauchos from twenty leagues around converge on a roundup to see and be seen. Some may merely sit and watch, but others will involve themselves in the excitement, showing off their accuracy with a lasso. See that bull over there? Watch me rope it by the left foot! They call this work?

Chapter 2
The Argentine National Character and Its Originality

The conditions of a cattle herder's life on the pampa create grave difficulties for any kind of political organization, especially for the triumph of European civilization, with all the liberty, prosperity, and institutional development which that civilization confers. On the other hand, one cannot deny that the pastoral life has its poetic side. If national literatures are able to shine forth in the new societies of America, it will be in the description of their grand natural environment and, above all, in the portrayal of the imposing struggle between European civilization and native barbarism, between intelligence and brute force. That struggle produces scenes and characters animated by an interior drama alien to the spirit of Europe, and therefore exceedingly unexpected to anyone educated within the normal circle of European ideas.

James Fenimore Cooper is the only North American novelist who has made a name for himself in Europe, and he did it in just that way, by moving the locus of his dramatic descriptions beyond the farming settlements, out to the wild frontier. There, Cooper shows the interaction between barbarism and civilization as Indians and settlers struggle perpetually for possession of the land.

1. Facundo: *The Shaping of a Paradigm*

The brilliant young Argentine poet Esteban Echeverría did something similar in his epic narrative poem "The Captive." Earlier Argentine poets had explored classical European themes quite creditably but without gaining a readership in Spain, and naturally enough, because they were really adding nothing new. Echeverría, on the other hand, turned his poetic gaze to the immense solitude of the pampa, solemn and overpowering, silent and unknowable, a setting completely unknown to Europe. And that way he began to gain readers outside of Argentina!

People around the world find like solutions to like problems. A similar natural environment produces a similar cultural response in widely separated peoples among whom no communication exists. The bow and arrow were invented, over and over again, by primitive people of all races, living on every continent of the globe. An Argentine reader of Cooper's frontier novels will recognize many behaviors of North American savages that are identical to the South American version. When surrounded by fire, an Argentine gaucho would do exactly what Cooper's frontiersmen do—create a firebreak ahead of the advancing flames. When Cooper describes a Pawnee preparing to cross a river, any Argentine understands that, skinning a buffalo, he will make an inflated buoy to carry him over the flood. Cooper's descriptions of Indian clothing, tools, and behavior could have been copied directly from observations made in South America.

Like religion, poetry is an inherent human faculty, and the grandeur of American environments naturally elicits a poetic response. Beauty and immensity, the known and the unknowable—these things stimulate the imagination. We do well to ask, about the average inhabitant of the Argentine pampa, what happens when he gazes toward the horizon and sees . . . nothing at all. The harder he looks, the more he sees nothing or, rather, something shifting, blurry and uncertain, something all the more fascinating because of its indeterminacy. What is out there? The gaze that goes constantly to the uncertain horizon must monitor it constantly to detect the approach of savages, danger, death. To live with one's eyes on that horizon is to live under threat.

A destructive thunderstorm can materialize at any moment. A dark cloud appears out of nowhere and expands quickly before the worried eyes of a traveler. With a thunderous crack a bolt of lightning strikes not far away, then another and another. Blinding light illuminates vast distances, alternating suddenly with claustrophobic darkness. Death is in the air, but so is the awesome spectacle of God's creation. When the storm passes, the gaucho continues on his way with the blinding

1. Facundo: The Shaping of a Paradigm

light burned onto his retina, as when one looks too long at the sun. The power of such experiences is undeniable, but how does the gaucho process them? Ask him about lightning and its dangers, and you will hear a mix of misinterpreted observations and ancient superstitions. On the pampa, just vigorously rubbing one's clothes produces a crackle of static electricity. It is well-known to nineteenth-century science that the human nervous system is sensitive to electricity. Imagine, then, the impact of living beneath an atmosphere so highly charged?

The gaucho's poetic sensibility is a natural result. All Argentines seem to possess a poetic sensibility. The poet Esteban Echeverría has garnered wide recognition for his sophisticated verse descriptions of our rivers that, like mother of pearl, reflect their emerald banks and the flitting, multicolored wings of pavas, picaflores, jilgueros, zorzales, and torcazas. Echevarría's poetry is the cultured, urban version of the gaucho's naive, spontaneous poetry, expressed primarily in song lyrics.

Just as every gaucho is a poet, every gaucho is a musician of sorts. The Argentine people's musical inclinations are well recognized by their South American neighbors. When, for the first time, an Argentine enters a house in Chile, his hosts will take him immediately to the piano or hand him a guitar, and if he is unable to play one or the other, they will profess amazement: "But aren't you Argentine?" This widespread notion, while not totally accurate, is nonetheless a telling indicator of Argentine national character. A young Argentine of good family will invariably play some musical instrument, piano or flute or violin, perhaps. On summer evenings, the common people gather at the door of the corner store to hear someone play the guitar and sing late into the night. Young men move in groups through the darkened streets, singing serenades at the windows of select young women. Men of mixed African and European descent frequently work as professional musicians and figure among the best-recognized composers and instrumentalists of the city of Buenos Aires.

Rural people have their own musical genres. The *triste*, as its meaning in Spanish suggests, is a chilling, plaintive, lyrical air, sung in the north of the Republic, a bleak music of the sort that Rousseau considers to be typical of primitive peoples. The *vidalita* is sung by groups of people in the street. I believe it to be of ecclesiastical origin, because I have heard it sung by Indians in northern Chile who probably learned it, in centuries past, from Spanish missionaries. These days gauchos use the *vidalita* as a musical accompaniment for improvised verses that tell the story of some recent skirmish in their neighborhood. The popular cultivation of these

1. Facundo: *The Shaping of a Paradigm*

two musical forms stands out among the otherwise rude and warlike customs of rural Argentina. Rough gauchos dressed in stinking, uncured leather get all dewy-eyed when they hear poetry. Echeverría tells of spending several months in the countryside back in 1840, when the fame of his poems already preceded him. The gauchos flocked to hear him, and if any one of them, ignorant of the young poet's identity, expressed skepticism of his "citified" dress and demeanor, the others would whisper in his ear, "Shhh . . . he's a poet."

The guitar is the most popular of instruments throughout South America, and very especially in Argentina. The city of Buenos Aires even retains the typically Spanish figure of the *majo*, a young guitarist whose playing is of particular delight to young women. Many young toughs who live on the outskirts of Buenos Aires play the guitar and sing in the manner of an Andalucian *majo*, and in the countryside, many young gauchos do something similar. Elements of style reveal a close relationship among these popular types—the way their wear their hats, their facial expressions, and the way they move their shoulders while singing, even the way they spit between their teeth! The Argentine genre called *cielito* retains the rhythmic energy of the Spanish *jaleo*, and Argentine performers snap their fingers in imitation of Andalucian castanets.

Any account of Argentine folk customs must include certain striking social types. Someday, no doubt, they will figure as protagonists of our national literature. I will describe only a couple of the most salient ones before going on to describe the origins, character, and impact of Argentina's incessant civil wars.

In Argentina, the most conspicuous, the most extraordinary social type of all is the tracker. To some degree, all gauchos are trackers. On plains so wide open, where paths crisscross, where cattle graze freely and horses amble in all directions, one must be able to recognize an animal's hoofprints, distinguish them from those of a thousand others, and follow them for miles. One must be able to know whether the animal is directing its own movements or being led, whether its pace is rapid or slow, whether it bears a burden or not. These are normal skills that all plainsmen must possess.

Once, when I was traveling with a guide across the plains, we came to a crossroads, and he studied the ground, as such men so often do, and said: "Here's a mule I know, an excellent saddle animal that belongs to Don N. Zapata. It was unsaddled yesterday, though, when it passed by here." The guide was coming from the Sierra de San Luis, and the mule train that had left the track was returning from Buenos Aires, hundreds

1. Facundo: *The Shaping of a Paradigm*

of leagues distant. The man had not seen the mule in question for a year, and now he recognized its hoofprints among those of an entire mule train that had passed along a trail two feet wide. This seemingly incredible but, nonetheless, far from unusual ability was demonstrated by a common herder, not a professional tracker.

The tracker by profession is a grave and circumspect personage whose declarations are accepted without question by local judges. His knowledge gives him a certain dignity and mystery in the eyes of others, who treat him with consideration, the poor because they fear him, the rich because they need him. Imagine that a theft has occurred during the night. As soon as it is discovered, people hurry to discover a footprint left by the thief, and upon finding one, they cover it with something so that the wind does not dissipate it. They call the tracker, who takes one look at the footprint and then sets off in the direction it indicates, hardly looking at the ground, as if his eyes register in high relief a trail imperceptible to everyone else. He walks down streets, crosses yards, enters a house, and pointing at a man inside it, says quietly: "It's him." The case is considered closed. It is a rare criminal, indeed, who dares challenge the tracker's verdict. The judge will consider it persuasive proof. To deny it would be unthinkable, absurd. The criminal bows to the testimony of the tracker as if it were the accusing finger of God himself.

I personally had the pleasure of meeting Calíbar, a famous tracker who exercised that profession in a certain province of Argentina for forty years. Today he is nearly eighty years old, and though stooped by age, remains venerable and dignified. Whenever someone mentions his fabulous reputation, he shrugs. "I'm old and worthless now, but there you have the children." These "children" are, of course, his grown sons, who exercise the profession that they learned from such a famous master.

The stories they tell about Calíbar! Once, when he was away on a trip to Buenos Aires, someone stole his best dress saddle and bridle. His wife found a footprint and covered it with a wooden bowl. Two months later, Calíbar returned, inspected what remained of the footprint, which was hardly anything, and nothing more was said about the matter—until a year and a half later, that is, when Calíbar came down a street on the edge of town, eyeing the ground, walked into a house, and found his saddle and bridle, now blackened and worn with use. He had finally picked up a trail almost two years old!

In 1830, a man condemned to death escaped from jail, and they called Calíbar. The escaped prisoner, certain that he would be tracked, had taken all the precautions that a fear of execution had suggested to

1. Facundo: The Shaping of a Paradigm

his mind—all of them useless! In fact, they may have further contributed to his demise, because Calíbar took them as a challenge to his reputation and outdid himself. The fleeing prisoner took advantage of every opportunity not to leave a trace of his passage. He went for entire blocks on tiptoe, crossed walled gardens, and doubled back repeatedly. Calíbar was right behind him. The prisoner walked a distance in the water of a drainage ditch and leapt out without leaving a footprint on the edge. Useless. Calíbar saw drops of water on the grass. The man climbed into a walled vineyard. Sometime later, Calíbar arrived, inspected the walls, and announced calmly: "He's inside." A squad of soldiers searched the vineyard and found nothing. "He didn't leave," said the tracker, without a second look. And he was right. The next day the fugitive was executed.

In 1831, certain political prisoners were planning their escape with the help of sympathizers on the outside. When all was in readiness, someone remembered: "What about Calíbar?" The others gasped, suddenly stricken and terrified: "Calíbar!" Fortunately for them, the political prisoners' families were able to persuade Calíbar to feign illness for four days following their escape, and thus they were able to get away without any difficulty.

What an amazing mystery! What can explain the microscopic eyesight of these trackers! How sublime is the creature that God created in his own image!

A second noteworthy social type of the Argentine pampa is the pathfinder. The pathfinder is a worthy individual who holds in his hands the fate of entire provinces. Invariably serious and reserved in demeanor, the pathfinder knows every bump and depression in twenty thousand square leagues of ground. The pathfinder's head holds a complete topographic map, the only map that most Argentine generals take with them on campaign. The pathfinder is always at the general's side, privy to all the military secrets; victory or defeat will depend on him. Perhaps no single thing contributes more to the general's peace of mind than confidence in his guide. Does another path go to the left? The pathfinder will know to what remote watering hole the path leads. And the next, and the next, for days and days. He will know where rivers can be forded, and where they can't, and how to pick a path safely through this patch of swampy ground, and that patch. And so on, and on. The pathfinder knows distances, how far every place on the pampa is from every other place in the number of days of travel time.

On the pampa, the pathfinder scans the horizon carefully, observes the lay of the land, then goes straight to his destination as the crow flies, even though it may be several days' and nights' travel distant. In the darkest,

1. Facundo: The Shaping of a Paradigm

most starless night the pathfinder can determine the direction of travel by examining the grass, pulling up handfuls to taste the leaves and smell the roots. Then the pathfinder remounts, says with self-assurance, "We're headed in the right direction," and continues unhurriedly on his way. Acting sometimes as his own pathfinder, Rosas impresses his gauchos by displaying just these sorts of expertise when he campaigns on the southern pampa of Buenos Aires.

At the approach of enemy forces, the pathfinder can let his general know their distance and direction long before they have become visible. The trick is to observe the flightless pampa rhea and other small animals whose movements show alertness to a large group of approaching horsemen.[6] Then, when a smudge of dust barely appears on the horizon, the pathfinder can begin to estimate the strength of the enemy force: "It's two thousand of them," he says, or "just two hundred," and the general responds accordingly, because the pathfinder will rarely be wrong. If condors or crows wheel silently in a corner of the sky, the pathfinder will decide whether they have spotted hidden enemies, a recently abandoned camp, or simply a dead horse.

If all this seems exaggerated, think again. Consider the example of the Uruguayan general Fructuoso Rivera who, like Rosas, has pathfinder pretensions of his own. Rivera is said to know every bush and tree in the entire Republic of Uruguay. Military victories there seem always to depend on his intervention. Rivera got his start as a pathfinder back in 1804 when he led parties of frontier contrabandists fighting Spanish colonial authorities. Then he switched sides to serve the Spanish king, who wanted to control the contrabandists. Then he switched sides to support the patriots who were rebelling against the king. Then he joined the Brazilians who invaded Uruguay. Then he collaborated with the Argentine army that expelled the Brazilians. And now he is in a position to thwart the current attempt by Rosas to control Uruguay militarily, all because of Rivera's indubitable talents as a pathfinder.

Then there is the *gaucho malo*, a sort of neighborhood tough, more misanthropic and ornery than bloodthirsty or bad. Imagine Cooper's Hawkeye character, his backlands know-how and aversion to town life, but without Hawkeye's natural morality or connections to the Indigenous people. The nickname *gaucho malo* is not meant to be entirely unfavorable and is pronounced with fear and even respect, not hatred. The lawmen have been chasing him for years. He has no fixed abode, but rather lives

---

6. The rhea looks similar to the ostrich, though it is smaller.

1. Facundo: The Shaping of a Paradigm

wherever he unsaddles his horse for the night, making a supper of small game or, if he's really hungry, taking down some rancher's cow to eat the tongue, which he considers the greatest delicacy, and leave the rest of the carcass for the vultures. Stock rustling is his worst habitual offense. He plays a game of hide-and-seek with the ten-soldier troop of local mounted police. No sooner have the soldiers left a given locality than the gaucho malo appears, to be greeted warmly and without surprise by the gauchos buenos, who gather around him admiringly. While in town, the gaucho malo buys tobacco and a few other store-bought necessities. If the local constabulary reappears, the gaucho malo slowly remounts and, without hurry, without so much as looking directly at the approaching soldier, rides out of town. Evidently they don't intend to try to arrest him today.

Or, if they care to try, let them! The soldiers are disinclined to try. Their government-issued horses cannot compare with the gaucho malo's famous horse. With any head start at all, he will escape. When, by worse luck, he happens to get cornered by the police, the gaucho malo pulls out his long *facón*, his fighting and utility knife, and charges into the thick of the fight. Usually he slices his way out, with a few cuts to the platoon that was trying to arrest him, and lies flat on the back of his horse to dodge the bullets that come flying after him. When his pursuers finally give up the chase, the gaucho malo slows his horse to an amble, well satisfied with the outcome of the skirmish. Local poets will add it to the list of his triumphs, which are attracting attention, lately, across the breadth of the pampa. Reputation as a gaucho malo holds attraction for some heedless young women. The neighbors may see a gaucho malo appear at a dance one evening with a local girl on his arm. What! He must have stolen her from her parents! And, in fact, he has, or rather, convinced her to elope with him. The neighbors watch in amazement as he and the girl disappear into the moving lines of dancers. But the gaucho malo is a seducer whose promises are false. The next day he delivers the stolen young woman back to her family, lowering her from behind his saddle to the ground without even dismounting himself, ignoring the insults shouted by the girl's offended family, and riding back out onto the pampa.

This antisocial outlaw, this white savage, is not, at bottom, really worse than the townspeople, or at least not by much. The tough guy who attacks an entire troop of mounted police will commonly not molest travelers at all. His behavior expresses a certain mentality, an attitude toward authority. He is not a thief, excepting possibly as regards horses. Among gauchos, all things are possible regarding horses. For example, a rich rancher once asked our gaucho malo to locate a horse of an unusual

1. Facundo: *The Shaping of a Paradigm*

color, possessing certain extraordinary traits, and with a predetermined marking, a white star, on its shoulder. After a moment of silent meditation came the answer: "There is no such horse right now." This was not said impressionistically or dismissively. It did not refer to horses on offer here or there. Oh no. During the brief silence, this man had mentally reviewed thousands of animals which he had observed over the last few years, discarding those lacking the requisite color, traits, and marking. At the end of the process none remained. "No such horse" was not an opinion, but a finding.

The gaucho's memory for individual livestock is not so surprising. Human ingenuity follows human interests, whatever they may be. Napoleon was said to recognize two hundred thousand soldiers by their names. He depended on them and was said to remember details of the lives of each of them. Our gauchos likewise depend on their knowledge of horses.

Finally, there is the gaucho troubadour, whom we call a cantor. The figure of the cantor crystalizes the social division of Argentina between civilization and barbarism. The gaucho cantor is like a troubadour of medieval Europe. He travels from one place to another singing the praises of gaucho heroes. He carries news of events, births and deaths, marriages and battles. His songs would eventually be collected and interpreted by future historians, were it not for one inconvenient truth. The troubadour's medieval world exists parallel to another one, a modern, nineteenth-century world, infinitely more sophisticated and a much better source of sociological truth. Two societies exist simultaneously on the Argentine pampa: a modern society struggling to be born, still confined to the cities, and a medieval society that refuses to die, dominant in the countryside.

The gaucho cantor has no fixed abode. He spends the night wherever darkness falls. His home is wherever he finds a drink and an audience for his songs, wherever he strikes the opening chords of a *cielito* and couples rise to dance. Such places are not hard to find. Any place with liquor for sale and a group of horses tied around the doorway is likely to have a guitar hanging on the wall, ready to be placed into the hands of the arriving cantor. Most gauchos just won't drink, or won't drink much, if the music is not to their liking.

Their taste is not ours. They listen avidly to monotonous improvised narratives that circle back endlessly around metaphors of animals and images of pampas landscapes. The cantor possesses a repertory of popular verse forms—five-line stanzas, ten-line stanzas, various eight-line stanzas—and can interpret certain sentimental lyrics by request. Any number of these standard tunes embody noble emotions and speak well of the listeners'

1. Facundo: The Shaping of a Paradigm

preferences, although the overall level of quality is modest enough. The artistic high point of a cantor's performance normally occurs when his is chronicling the exploits of an aspiring gaucho malo. The pinnacle of excitement occurs when the exploits are those of the singer himself.

Like most self-respecting gauchos, the cantor occasionally finds himself pursued by the law. He may have accidentally killed a man or two during bar fights. Any gaucho has that kind of "bad luck" occasionally. And there will pretty certainly be episodes in which the cantor stole a much-desired pony or girl despite his better judgment and could not refrain, on subsequent occasions, from telling his listeners all about it.

That is exactly what happened on the banks of the Paraná River one day in 1840. A group of gauchos had spent hours listening to a cantor when sounds indicated the eminent arrival of a platoon of mounted police. The lawmen had taken the precaution of surrounding the music party on three sides, leaving open only the river side, where a high bank stood many yards above the churning Paraná. The cantor leapt on his horse and, draping his poncho over the horse's eyes so that it wouldn't be afraid, he spurred it toward the river, which it hit with an enormous splash after dropping a considerable distance through the air. The frustrated police and the former audience watched the cantor's horse surface a few seconds later and begin swimming strongly toward an island in the current, while his former rider lay stretched out face-up on the water in the horse's wake, holding the animal's tail with one hand, calmly watching the riverbank recede from view. A few police potshots raised small geysers to the left and right, only confirming that the fugitive would unlikely pay the ultimate price.

To the tracker, the pathfinder, the gaucho malo, and the gaucho cantor I could add more, equally curious, social types, but I will refrain from doing so. The four that I have already described are the keys to understanding the bloody civil conflicts that have torn Argentina apart in recent years. In coming chapters, readers will see how many of the country's political leaders, especially the informal war leaders called caudillos, embody these four social types writ large.

Chapter 3

Argentine Sociability: The *Pulpería*

Our first chapter sketched a man's education on the pampa, and that man has now come of age. His character has been shaped by the impulses of nature, not by society, for in practical terms none exists on the pampa.

1. Facundo: The Shaping of a Paradigm

He is independent but idle, and ready to enter the local microcosm of public life, the rural store, or *pulpería*.

The *pulpería* is above all a meeting place. It must never be forgotten that the pampa comprises, above all else, a pastoral society, a basic characteristic of which is widely dispersed population. The distances and small numbers of inhabitants distinguish pastoral societies from agricultural ones. Farmers sometimes live on the land they farm, but there is rarely much space between them. Their families, animals, and implements are in constant contact. Their products and the skills needed to produce them are varied; some sort of village center and commons will be essential. Intensive farming requires abundant labor. On farms, the sons of the farmer will rarely be idle.

Life on the pampa contrasts with this situation absolutely. Each ranch house is separated from the others by many miles of open countryside. Women do all the domestic work. The livestock require little care. The men take little interest in the administration of their properties. They are bored. The one activity from which they have never flinched is riding horseback. Time to ride over to the *pulpería* and see what is going on. That is where they will end up, but men often set out with no particular destination in mind. Perhaps they intend vaguely to take a look at a newborn calf, and then later you find them at the *pulpería*.

Boys bring horses to the corral for saddling first thing in the morning, and every man will saddle one, even if he has no plans to go anywhere. A saddled horse is an integral part of a rural man in Argentina, as indispensable to his person as his urban counterpart's necktie. "He and his horse appear to be a single being. He lives on horseback, haggles and buys and sells on horseback. He eats and drinks and sleeps and dreams on horseback." Those words were written by Victor Hugo, but they could have been written on the pampa. The war leader called El Chacho summed up the gaucho's idea of total misery when asked, upon his escape to Chile, how he was doing. "How am I doing? How do you think? In Chile . . . and on foot!"

At the *pulpería* there will be other rural men with whom to commiserate. At the *pulpería*, the virtues of horseflesh and the probable whereabouts of missing animals and the current hunting grounds of major predators are discussed. The outlines of various cattle brands are traced in the dirt floor. Challenges for future horse races are issued and accepted. And, if someone is buying drinks, a gaucho *cantor* will be offering songs.

On the pampa, the society of the *pulpería* replaces larger, more general forms of sociability. At the *pulpería*, liquor lights up atrophied

1. Facundo: *The Shaping of a Paradigm*

imaginations and gambling stimulates benumbed emotions. The daily participants in the *pulpería* conversations become the arbiters of local reputations in the neighborhood. A gaucho esteems courage, physical prowess, and riding ability above all else, and he looks to the gathering at the *pulpería*, a bit like the chorus in a Greek drama, to formulate the collective assessment of each man's performance. For our purposes, it is interesting to notice how the attitudes that gauchos display at the *pulpería* structure their political behavior as well.

At the *pulpería*, as elsewhere, gauchos are given to trials of strength using their knives. Spanish men are known for their knife play, but Argentines outdo them. More than as a weapon, the knife serves gauchos as an all-purpose tool. A gaucho cannot live without his knife any more than the elephant could live without his trunk. Pretty much all gauchos want to be known for their boldness in knife play, just as all want to be known as skillful horsemen. At the least provocation, or with none at all, they draw their blades and flash them in the air, playfully throwing practice jabs as if shaking and throwing dice. Knife fighting is so routine an activity that many consider it the only way to settle any kind of disagreement or rivalry. Whereas men in other countries seize a knife with the intention of killing, the Argentine gaucho intends only to try his strength and ability, and the first to draw blood is the winner. Only a man who is very drunk or insane with rage will try to kill his adversary in such a fight. His objective, on the contrary, is to "mark" his adversary with a superficial cut that leaves a lasting scar, ideally on the loser's face, as a permanent advertisement of the winner's triumph. A circle of spectators forms around the dueling pair to witness the outcome, but no effort to separate the fighters precedes the spilling of blood. Blood ends the contest, unless there is a misfortune, a *desgracia*, they call it, when one of the fighters gets carried away or kills the other by accident.

The spectators' sympathies then go to the gaucho who has suffered the misfortune of killing unintentionally. Despite the general sympathy for men who suffer this misfortune, there will be legal consequences. A sympathetic onlooker may offer the unfortunate killer a particularly fast horse with which to make his escape. Friends in a distant neighborhood will shelter him, no doubt, if he can outrun the local mounted police. If the police catch up with him and he fights and defeats them, the unfortunate killer may have the beginnings of a regional reputation. Let enough time pass, and the unfortunate killer will be able to return to his rural neighborhood and live quietly. Only a string of killings is regarded as evidence of bad character. As a private rancher, Juan Manuel de Rosas extended

1. Facundo: The Shaping of a Paradigm

his protection to any number of men wanted for homicide. What Rosas won't tolerate on his property is a poor man accused of stealing.

Is the quotidian background of political power in the Argentine Republic becoming clearer? Consider the games of horsemanship and type of daring that they encourage. In one, a gaucho rides at full speed while a friend trips up his horse, throws the bolas to entangle its legs, so that the animal goes down in a cloud of dust, and out of the cloud runs the gaucho, who has landed on his feet. Is this the sort of leader one wants?

Because this is precisely the sort of man who gains positions of leadership on the pampa. Perhaps you believe that I am exaggerating. It is obviously not the case that every equestrian athlete ends up as a knife-wielding tough guy. Thousands of such local heroes meet an obscure end as small-time bandits engaged in an eternal game of hide-and-seek with the police. But hundreds of others exercise authority today in the Argentine countryside. Natural talent is always wastefully diverted by despotism. Men of natural capacity and ambition will find some outlet for their energies. If their social surroundings do not provide an outlet, those energies will find an antisocial outlet, which is what often occurs in rural Argentina, where civic culture and public life hardly exist. The gaucho malo who fights his police pursuers may become a regionally famous bandit, or, if political opportunities arise, he may lead an entire army in a civil war. The same skills are in play either way. To simplify just a bit, the gaucho with unusual ability will become a lawbreaker or a law enforcer, so that, in Argentina, breaking and enforcing the law become related activities.

Judges! Disobedient citizens require vigorous legal authorities. Argentine judges are nothing if not vigorous, although their actual legality is more questionable. Knowledge of law codes is not required, as the rural judge seldom applies them. His expertise lies not in legal niceties but in the liberal application of physical punishments, sometimes of his own devising. His greatest asset is a terrifying reputation. Not infrequently, today's judge is yesterday's much-feared desperado, finally obliged by age to abandon sleeping in the open air and adopt a more distinguished lifestyle. In any case, his application of the law, if it can be called that, is totally arbitrary or, rather, guided entirely by his own passions. His sentences are unappealable. What the local judge does may not deserve the name "justice," but his authority remains unquestioned. There are some who exercise their authority for years and retire with excellent reputations, but they are not the majority. In most cases, the local population has unquestioningly obeyed the arbitrary, self-serving, dictates of the petty despot without

1. Facundo: *The Shaping of a Paradigm*

ever having believed in his pretentious justice. Thus does might, itself, make right in Argentine daily life.

Much of what I say about rural judges applies also to the provincial military commanders. The post of military commander is more important, however. The power to appoint military commanders lies with the government, so that one could say that it is an attribute of institutional, urban power. And yet the power is only apparent, not actual, because urban influence over the countryside is so weak. The gauchos are so difficult to control, one could say that only other gauchos can control them. The government finds itself obliged to appoint, as provincial military commanders, the sort of man who has already won the prestige of leadership in the rural milieu. In other words, institutional power is thereby extended to the winners of hundreds of local competitions for masculine preeminence. Buenos Aires cannot ever really impose itself on the interior, one could say, except by endorsing the power of existing provincial caudillos. They hope to co-opt the caudillo's influence, but the plan often backfires, further along, when the caudillo refuses to obey orders from the capital. Thus do the provincial military commanders become the presidential heirs apparent of the Argentine Republic. It is not a coincidence that all the major Argentine caudillos to emerge from the revolution—including Artigas, Güemes, Facundo, and Rosas himself—began their ascent as provincial military commanders.

The urban attempt to co-opt rural power has failed spectacularly, producing a power inversion in which rural barbarism dominates urban civilization. Readers may object that I give too much importance to the details of political careers, that I demean the political process by downplaying the importance of ideals and ideologies. Such readers will be applying their imported ideas to Argentine realities, and the inevitable result will be a failure of interpretation, the way that European travelers looked at a jaguar and misunderstood it, in Old World terms, as a "tiger." Political ideals and ideologies are merely window dressing in the daily commerce of Argentine power. Masculine values of dominance within a particular social and cultural framework—that is the actual stock in trade. The framework that I have described is rarely foregrounded, but it is invariably functional in the background. It is not peripheral to the system but, rather, the heart of it.

With that in mind, we can correctly interpret the general evolution of Argentine political life since the beginnings of our struggle for national independence in 1810. Two distinct and incompatible ways of life already existed in Argentina before that year, one that we can easily identify as European, urban, and cosmopolitan, the other, of a much more local color, something partly Indigenous, thoroughly barbarous, distinctively American. The revolution of 1810 stirred the pot, bringing these two ways of life into contact with one another. Conflict between them was immediate. After years of fighting, the triumph of civilization over barbarism was to be expected, but it did not occur. Instead, by the mechanism that I have outlined, the ethos of the barbaric countryside gained systematic ascendency over the ethos of European civilization.

Add, now, add the peculiar education of men in the pampa milieu. Factor in the sort of heedless and aggressive persona that normally acquires a dominant reputation in the local *pulpería*. Now imagine that, attracted by who knows what sort of talk, the gauchos gather at hundreds of local *pulperías*, each with its own tracker and pathfinder, its gaucho malo and its gaucho cantor, its judge and its military commander. They have been born of the revolution, but other than that, their political color is murky. Their leadership and general enthusiasm, however, are clear. These makeshift militias constitute the provincial montoneras,[7] and their most powerful leader is Facundo Quiroga of the Province of San Juan.

The apotheosis of the montoneras brought with it, ultimately, a central government, one located in the city of Buenos Aires but representative of the countryside, a government that today has cast aside centuries of cultural progress to invert the normal preeminence of civilization over barbarism, balancing the fate of Argentina on the blade of a gaucho *facón*.

Chapter 5
The Life of Juan Facundo Quiroga

L'homme de la nature n'a pas encore appris à contenir ou déguiser ses passions.[8]

Between the cities of San Luis and San Juan lies a broad desert so bleak and parched that travelers call it "the crossing." The appearance of the place is quite forbidding, and travelers are careful not to pass the last

---

7. *Montonera* literally refers to a mounted group that played an often informal, yet central, role in military conflicts.
8. "The man of nature has not yet learned to contain or disguise his passions." From Alexandre Louis Félix Alix, *Histoire de l'empire Ottoman*.

1. Facundo: *The Shaping of a Paradigm*

watering hole without filling their canteens with the precious liquid. This was the setting, a few years ago, of the following scene.

A knife fight, as very frequently occurs among gauchos, had obliged one of the combatants to flee the city of San Luis on foot with his saddle on his shoulder. Two companions were to catch up with him as soon as they could steal horses for all three. Awaiting the man on foot, out on the sunburned desert crossing, were not only hunger and thirst, but also a man-eating "tiger." For a period of more than a year, this jaguar (for all American "tigers" are actually jaguars) had been preying on travelers in the crossing, and at this point it had eaten eight of them. By this time, the animal had developed a well-defined taste for human flesh, coming to truly deserve the name of man-eater.

After entering the crossing, the man fleeing on foot had gone six leagues when he heard the jaguar roar, sending a chill down his spine. The vocalization of a jaguar is unexpected. It might be confused at first with the grunting of a pig, but longer and more strident. Even if the hearer is unable to identify the source of the sound, even if he does not connect it with a killer feline, the jaguar's sound produces an instinctive shudder of dread, and this traveler was able to interpret it better than most. A few minutes later he heard another roar, considerably closer and clearer, obviously trailing him now. Scanning the horizon, the traveler found it uninterrupted—with one exception, a tall, slender carob tree standing completely by itself. The man walked faster and then began to run as the roars became louder and more frequent. Throwing his saddle on the ground he ran for the solitary carob tree, and despite the weakness of its slender (but fortunately elevated) trunk, was able to climb to, and partially conceal himself in, its branches. From there, as the tree swayed ceaselessly back and forth, he could watch the approach of the jaguar, coming quickly in the man's tracks, sniffing the ground, and emitting its weird vocalization with greater and greater frequency as it sensed the nearness of its intended prey. Passing the place at which the man had run for the carob tree, the jaguar temporarily lost the scent, whirled angrily, saw the discarded saddle, and tore it to shreds. Then, looking up, the animal saw the traveler in the slender, solitary, swaying carob tree, looking for all the world like an over-large bird perched on a sprig of cane.

The jaguar fell silent, leapt toward the tree, and, in the blink of an eye, reached two meters up the trunk with its claws, to set it swaying even more. Every shudder of the vibrating tree trunk struck terror into the heart of the trembling gaucho. The jaguar leapt vertically toward him, but the tree was too high. The animal paced around the tree roaring

1. Facundo: *The Shaping of a Paradigm*

furiously, and then, without taking its bloodthirsty eyes from the precariously perched gaucho, it flopped down, its dry mouth half-open, panting, its tail twitching in the dust.

Two hours passed without any substantial modification to this scene. The gaucho clutched the still-swaying branches in a position difficult to maintain indefinitely. His terrified eyes were riveted on the ravenous jaguar, and terror was gradually consuming his strength. His trembling fingers seemed about to lose their grip when a distant rumor of galloping horses restored his hopes. His friends had seen the jaguar's tracks and followed them at full speed, though without much confidence in being able to rescue him until they saw him in the swaying carob tree. The gauchos lassoed the jaguar, inviting its intended victim to descend and finish the animal with his knife. "I was happy to do it. That was the day that I learned about fear," said General Juan Facundo Quiroga, upon recounting this anecdote to a group of his officers. "Tiger of the Pampa" they called him, in later years, and the name rather suited him.

The modern nineteenth-century sciences of phrenology and comparative anatomy have demonstrated a close correspondence between physical characteristics and one's behaviors and moral compass.[9] We need a physical description of the man whom, for a long time, the people of the Argentine interior called simply Facundo. His excellency Brigadier General Don Facundo Quiroga got those fancy titles only after the country embraced him and crowned him with laurels. Facundo was short and muscular. His wide back and thick neck supported a well-formed head covered with black, curly hair. His pallid oval face contrasted with the surrounding hirsute forest, including a black beard that ascended almost to his prominent cheekbones. Facundo's dark eyes blinked beneath bushy black eyebrows. It was unnerving to talk with him because he never looked at anyone directly. Instead, he tended to incline his head, as if watching the ground, and peer at his interlocutors occasionally through his eyebrows, as if planning to ambush them at the first opportunity. In phrenological terms, an examination of the caudillo's skull would reveal the bone structure of a man accustomed to giving orders. Men with that sort of character will develop according to the cultural milieu in which they are born. Conditions favorable to their development will produce a

---

9. Phrenology was a combination of scientific practices and thinking that in the nineteenth century sought to link intellectual ability and potential, as well as personality traits, to the shape and features of a person's skull and scalp. Through its rise and fall, phrenology exercised enormous influence in scientific thinking and popular culture.

1. Facundo: The Shaping of a Paradigm

superior man, a man among men, whereas unfavorable conditions will produce a travesty, a barbaric throwback such as Facundo Quiroga.

Quiroga's father was a poor but honest man of San Juan who managed to assemble quite a fortune raising livestock on the plains of La Rioja. In 1799, the boy Facundo was sent back to San Juan to learn to read and write, which was as much education as anyone could get there at the time. Anecdotes about him in this period abound. His boyish behavior may not warrant so much attention, but some anecdotes do seem to paint a psychological portrait of the man he later became. For example, they say that he never once sat down to eat at the table with the other men who lived at the boarding house. At school, he was a loner. He rarely socialized with the other students, rarely had anything to do with them, in fact, except for a few occasions when he got into fights with them or instigated some mischief in which he became the ringleader.

The schoolmaster had his hands full with Facundo. At one point, he got a heavy, fearsome-looking, new whip and showed it to the class, explaining, "This is to try on Facundo." Facundo, who was eleven years old at the time, did not keep the schoolmaster waiting for an opportunity to try out the whip. The very next day he volunteered to recite the lesson directly to the teacher, rather than to the teaching assistant who normally heard the students recite what they were assigned to memorize. Facundo had, in fact, not studied his lessons any more than on other occasions. But he had studied the situation, including the weakness of the wobbly chair where the teacher sat to hear recitations. Facundo committed a first error, then a second and a third, and then the teacher raised his new whip when Facundo committed another error, which was the fourth and final error of the recitation that day. Facundo's fist sent the teacher over backward as the chair collapsed and the disobedient student disappeared into a vineyard, where he hid for the next three days.

Perhaps the reader can discover, in this anecdote, the caudillo who would one day defy an entire society?

At puberty, Facundo's character takes on more pronounced, and darker, tints. He becomes ever more imperious and barbaric. Gambling—the pastime of rough, insensitive spirits that tend to grow dormant without powerful stimulation—became his passion from the age of fifteen. Gambling makes the boy's reputation among the townspeople, gambling gets him evicted from the house where he was boarding, and, by means of a bullet that killed a fellow gambler named Jorge Peña, it leads him to spill his first blood, as well. Peña's is only the first rivulet of a torrent of blood that will mark Facundo's time on earth.

1. Facundo: *The Shaping of a Paradigm*

His movements as a young adult are impossible to trace with precision, but the sum of them adds tidily to the overall picture. He did not stray far from his original stomping ground but appeared haphazardly in a neighboring area, then in a nearby town, then somewhere else, always gambling, skulking through the countryside, leaving a trail of stab wounds among the gauchos who dared to challenge him, and was generally employed, or half employed, or (it is more accurate to say) officially employed as a peon on this or that ranch. In San Juan, the Godoy family displays stamped earth walls, called *tapias*, that they proudly claim were built by none other than Facundo Quiroga. And there is little reason to doubt them because he apparently constructed many tapias in the region at this time. In Fiambalá, Province of La Rioja, there are others. On the occasion when he executed twenty-five of the officers who had surrendered to him at Chacón, Quiroga stood them up against tapias that he had made as a young man, at least according to his explanation at that moment. And he had similar monuments to his laboriousness in Buenos Aires Province.

Now, building a tapia is dirty, brutish shovel work. What had caused this young man, the son of a well-off family of decent reputation, to descend to the level of a common laborer and then to specialize in the dirtiest, most brutish occupation commonly practiced in the countryside of Argentina? The most probable hypothesis seems to be that a builder of tapias received more money, and Facundo needed money to fuel his passion for gambling.

That passion played a determining role in this obscure period in the future caudillo's life. In 1816, Facundo was put in charge of a train of pack mules carrying cochineal dye over the Andes from San Juan to Chile. The cochineal belonged to his father, as did the mules and the mule drivers, who were his father's slaves. Now, Facundo had often been sent to Chile, before this time, with herds of cattle from his family's properties. But neither before, nor in 1816, could he refrain from heedlessly gambling away the family property entrusted to his supervision, and his father finally lost patience, leading to a permanent estrangement between the incorrigible young man and his long-suffering parents.

Once, when Facundo had already become the terror of the Republic, one of his many flatterers asked about his biggest bet ever. "It was a seventy-peso bet," replied Facundo without thinking about it. A mere seventy pesos? How so? At the moment of the conversation, he had just won a pot worth two hundred ounces of gold! Seventy pesos? Yes, because it was everything he had at the time. He had been working for a woman

1. Facundo: *The Shaping of a Paradigm*

who owned a large property in Mendoza, and, in the course of a year's labors, Facundo had emerged as her most punctual and responsible peon, and the one who exercised the most influence over the others. For example, when the other peons wanted to skip work and do some binge drinking, Facundo persuaded them not to do so without advising the owner. He spoke to her directly about their plans, promising to make sure all her peons would show up the following day, which they always did, without fail. His workmates made fun of his propriety, calling him Father Facundo. In other words, the future caudillo's exiguous wages were well earned.

After a year, Facundo asked for all his accumulated earnings, which amounted to no more than seventy pesos, and rode off, with no particular destination in mind, according to his own telling of this story. Passing a *pulpería*, he saw a crowd of gauchos engaged in a game of cards. He gave his year's wages to the dealer, losing it all on a single bet. With a shrug of his soldiers, he got back on his horse and rode aimlessly, until he encountered a local judge by the name of Toledo. The judge made the fatal error of asking Facundo to show his employment papers. In Argentina, vagrancy laws require gauchos to be employed and to carry a certification of employment. Facundo pretended to search for his papers, but what he found was his *facón*, and he left the judge lying in his blood. This gratuitous, thoughtless killing challenges us to understand the mentality of the killer. Was Facundo acting out his frustration at the loss of his year's wages? Was he burnishing his reputation as a gaucho malo? Probably both. Facundo showed a frequent tendency to vent anger at innocent bystanders. He once condemned a young man to two hundred lashes, almost a death sentence, for having told a joke when the caudillo was in no mood for joking. Unbelievably, he condemned a woman to the same brutal punishment for greeting him on the street when he was in no mood for greetings.

Facundo's military career began in Buenos Aires, where we find him in 1810, joining patriot forces about to begin their glorious march to Upper Peru. With a bit more discipline to keep him on track and a noble cause to direct his butcherous instincts, he might well have returned from the war as a victorious general. In just that way did the wars of independence raise many a humble gaucho to a position of rank and honor—but not Facundo. He could not endure the discipline of the barracks, the wait for eventual promotions, or any other form of military subordination. He wanted to impose himself, not in accordance with existing norms, but in defiance of them. He was recruited for the Army of the Andes and the

1. Facundo: *The Shaping of a Paradigm*

Horse Grenadiers but deserted long before winning any patriotic glories. In later years, both Facundo and Rosas showed undying animosity toward patriot veterans, slaughtering them on more than one infamous occasion.

The deserter Facundo left Buenos Aires with three cronies. Pursued by the police, they killed four or five of their pursuers and continued in a westward direction until finally arriving at the house of Facundo's parents in San Juan. Here the caudillo's legend includes a dark chapter indeed. According to most tellers of this tale, Facundo demanded money from his father and mother, who refused to give it. He supposedly waited until both parents were asleep, locked them in their bedroom, and set the house on fire. Houses on the Argentine plains typically have thatched roofs, and nothing burns hotter or faster. I would prefer not to credit these accounts, which seem too horrible to be true. Among the many manuscripts that I perused in researching the caudillo's life, I did find a quotation to the effect that "there is no proof that Facundo ever robbed his parents using threat of violence." However, I subsequently received testimony that tends to confirm the account of Facundo's murder of his own parents. A childhood companion of the caudillo's recounted having seen Facundo strike his father and run away. Another witness recounted having personally heard Facundo tell the story of setting fire to his parents' house.

There can be no doubt of the following. Facundo's father once petitioned the provincial government of La Rioja, asking that his son be arrested to prevent his totally running amok. The boy learned of his father's petition and assaulted him, daring him to take further legal action, before disappearing at a gallop onto the open pampa. A year later, he appeared at his father's house and, throwing himself at his father's feet, he begged for forgiveness. The old man was willing to give it, and for a time, at least, peace was restored between them.

But the young man did not mend his ways. The obsession with cards and horse racing continued, the fights and knife play continued, and Facundo felt himself becoming unwelcome in all his familiar haunts. At that point, he had the brilliant idea of joining the montonera led by Francisco Ramírez. Of all the destructive montoneras rampaging through Argentina, this was among the most barbaric, the most criminal, the most opposed to urban civilization. The deserter from the glorious Horse Grenadiers, who had found a way to absent himself during the battles of Chacabuco and Maipú, had decided to express his patriotic sentiments by joining the montonera of Ramírez, and he made no secret

1. Facundo: The Shaping of a Paradigm

of it! Facundo's infernal plan seems to have dismayed even his friends, because they informed on him, leading to his arrest and imprisonment in San Luis. This occurred in 1818, at a moment when the prison at San Luis housed numerous Spanish prisoners of war who had been captured in Chile by San Martín. No sooner had Facundo been imprisoned than these Spanish officers staged a mass escape, and after freeing themselves, their next move was to free all the other prisoners, thinking to overwhelm the authorities with the sheer number of escapees. But no sooner had a Spanish officer removed Facundo's shackles, than the Argentine used them to break the officer's skull. Then, whirling a heavy iron chain, he opened a bloody path through the group of escaping Spaniards, killing no fewer than fourteen of them.

Other accounts mention different weapons and put the number of dead at only three, but Facundo's own version of this story never omitted the bloodied shackles and the number fourteen. The literal truth here is perhaps less important than the mythic content of this image, indicative of the kind of brute force so fervently admired on the pampa, an image with echoes of the imprisoned Sampson's revenge against his captors. Whatever weapon he used, Facundo's actions inspired other Argentine prisoners to join him, and together they foiled the Spaniards' attempt to escape. In one fell swoop, the disgraced small-time gaucho malo had restored his reputation and covered himself with patriotic glory. Suddenly famous, he was free to go, so he returned to the plains of La Rioja to exercise his well-deserved bragging rights as the killer of fourteen men in a single fight.

The character of Facundo Quiroga has been aptly summarized by a man who knew him as a boy, a man who provided me with detailed written information for this account and will, of course, remain anonymous for the sake of his own safety. In simple, candid language, he shows us an all-around picture of our subject, the potentially great man whose development was fatally twisted by his environment. "[Facundo] never stole anything as a private citizen, not even when in dire need, and he did not touch alcohol, but he dearly loved to fight and had a tremendous aversion to anything like a *gentleman*. He was never known to pray, go to confession, or hear mass from beginning to end, and he treated his followers like his personal servants. He wanted everybody to be afraid of him, and he pretended to possess psychic powers."

Offered a commission in the army, he scorns it as too limiting. He chafes at the idea of wearing a uniform and taking orders from officers who outrank him. The life of a roving gaucho, staying away from towns,

1. Facundo: The Shaping of a Paradigm

periodically fighting the police, has hardened his body and his spirit. He looks at the cities, their European civilization, their judges and law codes, with instinctive suspicion and scorn, even hatred.

Here, the chapter epigraph could not possibly be more pertinent. Our subject is "a man of nature," a primitive being totally in thrall to his emotions. His ego has never accepted any kind of subordination. In reaction to it, his fury knows no bounds. Enraged, he roars like a savage beast, and the serpentine curls of his black mane dangle around his head, Medusa-like. Enraged, he once kicked a gambling partner to death over a disagreement at dice. Incapable of winning people's respect, affection, and admiration in a positive way, he systematically terrorized everyone around him, whether soldiers or civilians, whether they were wretches awaiting execution or his own wife and children. Incapable of manipulating the levers of civil authority, he substituted terror for patriotism as his principal method of social control. Deeply ignorant of matters under his direction, he feigned omniscience and used his keen powers of observation to convince his even more ignorant, and also gullible, followers of his ability to predict the future.

The result is an endless repertoire of proverbial anecdotes about Facundo Quiroga, including famous quotations and actions that pass, among the common folk of the pampa, as examples of Solomonic wisdom. There was an occasion, often recounted, when Facundo identified a thief among his soldiers by cutting straws to an equal length and giving one to each man. "Tomorrow," he explained, "the thief will have the longest straw." The next day, however, one soldier's straw was *shorter* than all the others. Convinced that his straw would get magically longer in accord with the caudillo's prediction, the thief had preemptively shortened it and, in doing so, revealed his guilt. "You're the thief!" Facundo exposed the guilty party before the amazed eyes of his admiring followers. Solomon, in the famous biblical story, showed that he understood a mother's heart when he proposed that a disputed child be divided. Facundo showed he understood a different sort of heart. His followers believed that he could see right through them, so to speak. When someone stole parts of a gaucho's silver-inlaid bridle, and a complete search of saddle bags failed to recover it, Facundo assured his trembling followers that he could recognize the thief on close inspection, and he had them file past him, one by one, while he stood silently inspecting them with his arms crossed. Suddenly, he grabbed a gaucho by the sleeve and barked a question. "Where is the stolen bridle?" The thief confessed immediately and Facundo had him shot. Occasionally, he gave away the practical secrets behind his apparent sagacity, as when he interrupted a certain interrogation to say, "Stop, he's lying, a hundred lashes, next." When the guilty party had been led away, Facundo explained that "a gaucho who draws cattle brands with his toe while he talks—is always lying." On a fourth occasion, according to the storytellers, Facundo needed an audacious, capable man for a dangerous mission. The caudillo sat writing at his desk when they brought him a volunteer and, glancing up from the page, continued to write while indicating, with a dismissive toss of his black mane, the man should be removed from his sight. "Get him out of here. I asked for a brave man, and this is a coward." Needless to say, further investigation of the man's antecedents showed that the caudillo had recognized the truth instantaneously. Hundreds of such anecdotes can be heard today around pampas campfires.

This concludes our summary of Quiroga's private life. I have omitted countless further examples of his defective education, bloodthirstiness, and overall bad character. My goal has been to use these biographical elements to tell a larger political story. I have wanted to show the social origins of caudillos like Facundo Quiroga, how their milieu shaped them, and how they shaped the national political scene, producing the current Rosista dictatorship, through which the barbarous spirit of the pampa dominates the entire Argentine Republic.

Final Considerations
(Two passages from later chapters of *Facundo*)

The Federalist Party of the cities was able to dominate the Argentine Republic thanks to its alliance with the barbarous caudillos of the countryside against the revolutionary party of urban liberals. The liberals desired centralized political institutions such as those instituted by the French Revolution, whereas the barbarous caudillos desired to oppose whatever the urban liberals proposed. Therefore, when the liberals adopted the moniker Unitarians, the caudillos reflexively called themselves Federalists to take a contrary position, but it was a rhetorical tactic that belied a true understanding of a federal system. In fact, although these so-called Federalists lacked any real commitment to limiting centralized political control, they did have strongholds scattered across the interior provinces, and these were the forces unified by the leadership of Facundo Quiroga.

1. Facundo: *The Shaping of a Paradigm*

Argentine gauchos are quite provincial in outlook. They identify first with their province of origin—be it Santa Fe, Córdoba, or wherever—and only secondarily with the Argentine Republic as a whole. They view the populations of other provinces as unrelated tribes, as likely to be enemies as friends. Yet all shared a common interest in resisting the centralized control of Buenos Aires. The restless youth of Facundo Quiroga, during which he crisscrossed the provinces of the interior many times, equipped him to play a role in unifying them. Born in the Province of La Rioja, he had spent time in San Juan, Mendoza, and Buenos Aires as well. He had no primary attachment to any province. His overall perspective was national, rather than provincial. Once he took control of La Rioja, he was concerned with extending his prestige to the other scenes of his life, such as the city where he had attended school, the distant rural neighborhoods where he had built tapias or raged as a gaucho malo. Unlike other provincial caudillos, who were always reluctant to exercise their influence far from home, Facundo Quiroga was eager to do so. And thus do large matters of state sometimes stem from quirky and inconsequential causes.

❊ ❊ ❊

In the end, it was not the raging Riojano but his Buenos Aires ally, Juan Manuel de Rosas, who institutionalized power at the national level in Argentina. Among the things he institutionalized there was the climate of fear that Facundo had created so efficaciously. After the death of Facundo, the capital city lay supinely at the discretion of Rosas.

Imagine! The people of the city have candidly confirmed their surrender of all rights and institutions to the tyrant. The state is a blank slate for our genius. Upon it, like Plato, he will inscribe the outlines of the ideal republic upon which he has meditated for twenty years. Let us observe this prodigy. Leaving the legislature, where he received his staff of office, our creative genius withdraws in a coach painted red expressly for the ceremony. Yoked to the coach by cords of red silk are the men who, with criminal impunity, have kept Buenos Aires in a state of continual alarm since 1833. They style themselves The Society of the People. They wear knives, red vests, and red ribbons bearing the slogan "Death to the Unitarians." Arriving at the door of his house, these same men form an honor guard for the genius. He gives audiences to both generals and common citizens. Everyone must show their limitless personal loyalty to him, the so-called Restorer of the Laws.

1. Facundo: The Shaping of a Paradigm

The next day a proclamation appears with a list of proscriptions. This proclamation, one of the few writings done by Rosas himself, was a wonderful document that I am sorry not to have on hand. It was his program of government, undisguised and unambiguous. Whoever is not with me, is my enemy! Woe to those who provoke my fury! That is the axiom of policy enshrined therein. The document announced that blood would flow, that only property would be respected.

Four days later, the San Francisco parish church announced a celebratory mass, giving thanks to the Almighty for the rule of Rosas, inviting the people of the neighborhood to solemnize the event with their presence. The surrounding streets were dressed with banners and buntings, like a Middle Eastern bazaar displaying tapestries of purple and gold damask, and jewels in whimsical array. People thronged the streets, young people attracted by the novelty, ladies who had selected the parish of San Francisco for an afternoon stroll. The ceremony of thanksgiving was briefly postponed, protracting the general business and enthusiasm. The official gazette supplied the most insignificant details about the splendid event.

Eight days later, a second parish announces its own ceremony of thanksgiving. Its people are determined to surpass the official enthusiasm and outdo the decorations of the first parish. What ostentation of wealth and adornment! A portrait of "the Restorer" is placed on a dais in the street, swathed in red velvet, golden cords, and braid. The hubbub recommences. In the privileged parish, people seem to live in the street. And a few days later, there is another celebration, in another parish in another neighborhood.

How long can this go on? Do the people never tire of such spectacles? What sort of enthusiasm is this, that does not subside in a month? Why don't all the parishes hold their celebrations simultaneously?

No, no. This is a systematic, organized sort of spontaneity, administered a little at a time. A year later, all the parishes of Buenos Aires have still not concluded their celebrations. The official giddiness has passed from the city to the countryside. It appears endless. The government's gazette is occupied for a year and a half with descriptions of Federalist celebrations. The famous portrait of Rosas appears unfailingly, pulled along by generals, by ladies, by the purest of Federalists, in a carriage made especially for the purpose.

After a year and a half of celebrations, the color red emerges as the insignia of loyalty to "the cause." The portrait of Rosas first graces church altars, and then becomes part of the personal effects of each and every

1. Facundo: *The Shaping of a Paradigm*

man, who must wear it on his chest as a sign of "intense personal attachment" to the Restorer. Last, out of these celebration comes the terrible Mazorca, the corps of amateur Federalist police, whose designated function is to administer enemas of pepper and turpentine to dissenters, and next, should this prove insufficient, to slit the throat of whomever they are told.

All America has scoffed at these famous celebrations of Buenos Aires, seeing them as the maximum degradation of an entire people. What I see in them is a highly effective political strategy. How does one teach the idea of personalist government to a republic which has never had a king? The red ribbon is a token of the terror which now accompanies the people of Buenos Aires everywhere—in the street, and also in the bosom of the family. You must think of the red ribbon at least twice a day, when dressing and undressing. Human memory proceeds by association. The sight of a tree reminds us of the conversation we held underneath it a decade earlier. Imagine what ideas the red ribbon brings with it by association, the indelible impressions it has joined in our minds to the image of Rosas.

The story of the red ribbon is, indeed, curious. At first, it was an emblem adopted by partisans. Then they ordered everyone to wear it in order to "prove the unanimity" of public opinion. People meant to obey, but frequently forgot when they changed clothes. The police helped jog people's memories. The Mazorca patrolled the streets. They stood with whips at the church door when ladies were leaving Mass and applied the lash without pity. But there was still much which needed fixing. Was someone wearing his ribbon carelessly tied?—Must be a Unitarian! The lash!—Was someone's ribbon too short?—A Unitarian! The lash!— Someone did not wear one at all?—Some nerve! Cut his throat!

The government's solicitude for public education did not stop there. It was not sufficient to be a Federalist, nor to wear the ribbon. It was obligatory also to wear a picture of the illustrious Restorer over one's heart, emblazoned with the elegant slogan: "Death to the Savage, Filthy Unitarians!" Enough, you think, to conclude the job of debasing a civilized people, robbing them of all personal dignity? Ah! They were not yet well-enough disciplined. One morning, on a street corner in Buenos Aires, there appeared a figure drawn on paper, with a ribbon half a yard long floating in the breeze. As soon as some person saw it, that person backed away in fright and spread the alarm. People ducked into the nearest store and came out with ribbons half a yard long floating in the

1. Facundo: *The Shaping of a Paradigm*

breeze. Ten minutes later, the city's entire population was out in the street wearing ribbons half a yard long.

Another day, the figure reappeared with a slight alteration in the ribbon. The maneuver repeated itself. If some young lady forgot to wear a red bow in her hair, the police supplied one free of charge, and attached it with melted tar. That is how they have created uniformity of public opinion. Search the Argentine Republic for someone who does not firmly believe and maintain that he is a Federalist.

It has happened a thousand times. A citizen steps outside his door and finds that the other side of the street has been swept. A moment later, he has had his own side swept. The man next door copies him, and in half an hour the whole street has been swept, everyone thinking it was an order from the police. A shopkeeper puts out a flag to attract people's attention. His neighbor sees him and, fearing he will be accused of tardiness by Governor Rosas, puts out his own. The people across the street put up a flag, then the whole street, other streets follow suit, and suddenly all Buenos Aires is bedecked with flags. The police become alarmed and inquire what happy news has been received by everyone but them. And to recall that this feckless population trounced English soldiers and sent five armies across the continent during our wars for independence!

Terror, you see, is a disease of the spirit which can become an epidemic like cholera or scarlet fever. No one is safe, in the end, from the contagion. Though you may work ten years inoculating them, not even those already vaccinated can resist steady fear. Do not laugh, nations of Spanish America, when you witness such degradation. Look well, for you, too, are of Spanish descent, and this fear of inconformity is what the Inquisition taught us Spaniards. This sickness we carry in our blood.

2. *Facundo*'s Impact

The following selections allow readers to glimpse the initial impact of *Facundo*. Whether in Sarmiento's own reflections published in newspapers, or through news reports of one of the many translations of the essay done during Sarmiento's lifetime, the ramifications of *Facundo* extended far and wide. Sarmiento targets Rosas specifically in a column on Camila O'Gorman—a young woman who fell in love with a priest, became pregnant, and then was killed with her lover by firing squad at Rosas's orders. Camila's story complements *Facundo* and the film *Camila*, for those instructors who assign it. Simply put, long before this essay became a staple in Latin American studies courses, the core ideas of Sarmiento's argument had influenced intellectuals as well as political and military leaders across Latin America. *Facundo*'s context was local, but its impact, applications, and analysis took on a life of their own, often extending far beyond Argentina.

❋ ❋ ❋

"My Books," from *Recuerdos de Provincia*, first published in 1850

Civilization and Barbarism. I wrote this book to make Chileans aware of Rosas and his politics. I intended that it be the product of careful meditation, enriched with historical data and documentation. Instead, every page bears marks of its hasty composition, publication having begun while the book was still being written, amid the disappearance

2. Facundo's Impact

of irreplaceable sources. The book established my honorable reputation in Europe, at least, according to the prestigious *Revue des Deux Mondes*.

Following the initial publication in the Chilean *El Progreso*, *Facundo* came off the presses of the Montevideo newspaper *El Nacional* and has been translated into German with illustrations by Rugendas.[1] One can say that Europe's general understanding of conflict in the Argentine Republic has been based for years on *Civilization and Barbarism*. The book contains the starting point of many others which, taken together, have blackened the name of Rosas in the eyes of enlightened people everywhere.

Rosas himself regards the book as an effective antidote to his misguided policies. He has made its efficacy clear by omission. During five years of abusive insults directed toward me by his obedient press organ, *The Mercantile Gazette* of Buenos Aires, the title of my book has never once appeared, even though over five hundred copies are circulating in Argentina. Every Rosas ally of any significance has already read it and probably possesses a copy. The book remains among the most avidly sought and read in the country. Rosas never mentions it, pretending never to have heard of it, in a vain attempt to limit the book's notoriety.

Here's what the *Revue des Deux Mondes* has to say about my book (and its author) in an article on "Americanism and the Republics of the South: Argentina": "During his stay in Chile, which preceded his European travels, Sarmiento published his brilliant study *Civilization and Barbarism*—rich in color and images, as instructive as a history, as interesting as a novel. It is a precious document, a rare opportunity for us to explore the intellectual life of South America. . . . More than one of its vigorous pages were dictated by the author's fiery political passions, and yet, such are his intellectual fairness and talent that, even at the book's most passionate, he gives to people their true character, and to the social context, its natural color. . . . South American affairs can be just as interesting, when shrewdly analyzed, as those of the United States. It is a task for travel writers and philosophers, for poets and historians. Señor Sarmiento has begun the task in this book first published in Chile. It shows that civilization may have enemies in South America, but fortunately, it does not lack for eloquent South American friends."

Obras, vol. 3, p. 211

---

1. German painter Johann Moritz Rugendas traveled throughout Latin America, living in different areas for years. He illustrated scenes of daily life, travel books, and translations.

2. *Facundo's Impact*

"On the Appearance of *Facundo* in Italian Translation," in *El Nacional,* 22 September 1881

Announcing the publication, in Italian translation, of the book whose lyricism inspired in many readers the sort of exaltation that becomes chronic among persons exiled from their homes for religious or political reasons, a sort of somnambulism by which Garibaldi or Moses guided their followers to the Promised Land. The vision is internal, rooted in their passionate hearts, but the guides imagine it to be external, surrounded by a nebulous aureola that makes it appear near at hand when, in fact, it always marches ahead, out of reach, like a desert mirage. Its vague beauty attracts us onward until death or disenchantment finally breaks the illusion.

The discoverer Columbus glimpsed a wonderland covered with virgin forests, tangled with hanging vines, animated by songs and sonorous colors, alive with myriad hymns arising from serpents, birds, volcanoes, and waterfalls, each speaking in its own voice. The Italian patriot Mazzini died, like Joshua, upon emerging from his desert wanderings to see the image of Italian greatness rising up beyond the snowy peaks of the towering Alps. Another Italian, Pedro de Angelis, said of *Facundo,* "There is movement here, like waves of tall grasses undulating on the pampa, exuding a bitter smell. The statesman Avellaneda recalls reading the book as a beardless university student in Córdoba, back in the days when intellectual stagnation hung heavy in the atmosphere. For him, *Facundo* lit up the night like a shooting star, leaving its bright trail on his retinas even after the return of darkness. The Chilean minister Barros Arana, crossing the pampa on his way to Tucumán, announced upon attending the inauguration of a railroad: "The political atmosphere has changed. Books like *Facundo* will nevermore be written in Argentina." Neophytes and doctors of laws agreed in saying of the book: "I read it at a single sitting."

Most Argentines had little to say about the book, however. Possibly they saw it as a homely native plant that normally passes unremarked in its normal habitat, like the cactus of the Argentine countryside, until one day an enterprising botanist cultivates it as an exotic adornment for European gardens. Or perhaps the book failed to impress provincial readers whose literary taste remained too focused on Cervantes, like those who remain unimpressed by the gothic architecture of France because it isn't mentioned in *Don Quijote*.

The most influential readers of *Facundo* were outsiders: Lewis, the English professor of the University of Buenos Aires, steeped in the language of Shakespeare; Mazade, the Frenchman who interpreted the book for the countless authors who publish in the *Revue des Deux Mondes*. A French mariner translated it with footnotes clarifying passages or allusions that he feared might otherwise remain ill understood. A young North American crossed the pampa with a train of oxcarts and, upon arriving in San Juan, made his way through the book with difficulty. He continued on to China and there penned his fervent appreciation of my efforts. In the United States, Mrs. Horace Mann whisked the manuscript away to translate it, and I recovered it only in time to prevent her from adding a book-length biographical preface. Nonetheless, Gaston Maspero recently declared that no translation can really do *Facundo* justice.

So, let the book stand with all its imperfections forever unrevised. Its contemporaries considered it a brilliant triumph, especially readers far from Argentina. Today, thanks to *Facundo*, our Argentine pampa awakens poetic associations for distant readers not dissimilar to those surrounding the Scottish highlands described by Sir Walter Scott. And it is well to remember, forty years after the book's appearance, that it also served to help bring down a tyrant. The tyrant Rosas was overcome by the weight of public opinion, made unfavorable to him throughout the civilized world by my peculiar and ill-formed little progeny.

Enough about the past! Sancho Panza, my faithful squire and shield bearer, reach me my spurs, for methinks that this old knight-errant still has time for a last expedition to right what's wrong, and straighten what's twisted.

Obras, vol. 46, pp. 320–24

"The Case of Camila O'Gorman,"
in *Crónica* [Santiago, Chile], 26 August 1849

Amid the monotony of daily life there occur, every now and then, scandalous events that stir the spirit and awaken curiosity far and wide. A secret empathy links all people who recognize their common vulnerability to crimes of passion that seem everywhere similar, arising, as they do, from analogous situations. Thus the entire world has avidly followed the developments surrounding the cases of Madame Defarge, the Duke of Praslin, and Frère Leotade as reported in the French press. It is natural to

2. Facundo's Impact

desire the triumph of justice and the repression of the vengeful passions that the criminals had sought to erase along the road that led to the crime. It is a relief finally to see justice done to criminals who appeared confident that they would evade it.

These ideas have occurred to me while reading a brief pamphlet titled *The Murder of Camila O'Gorman*, chronicling an occurrence which took place in Buenos Aires several months ago and became the subject of frequent reporting in the newspapers there. But reading about the case of Camila O'Gorman produced a totally contrary effect when compared with the aforementioned accounts of justice done. Here justice seems entirely absent, not even sought, and its judicial representatives, instead of impressing us with their sagacity and resourcefulness, seem more like the real criminals themselves.

It is commonly reported that Buenos Aires today is a quiet and orderly city, with vigorous maritime connections and commerce of all kinds. Just off the boat, European visitors, merchants, and businessmen of all stripes concur that the city provides a profitable venue for their manifold activities.

Just below the surface of daily life, however, circulate more subtle currents that it might take years for the casual visitor to learn to observe. For example, medical doctors have reported a rapid, and thus far totally unexplained, rise in cases of tuberculosis, and anyone who enters the houses of many families in the city will witness a second hidden plague, hundreds of insane persons whose madness is carefully concealed from the public gaze. The cause of the madness is less obscure than the cause of the tuberculosis, for many of the insane are ardent young men whose frustrations have left them in a sort of stupefied withdrawal from the world. The terrible scenes of violence that they have witnessed, the horrible emotions that they have felt, and the gradual frustration of all their hopes have left these unfortunates utterly nullified. Many physicians believe that the tuberculosis, too, may correspond to similar psychological causes, chronic fear, and the need to constantly hide it, because repressed human emotions damage the physical body when they are not allowed any sort of expression.

The same phenomenon of chronic repression and its consequences may be observed in the social behavior of respectable families in the city of Buenos Aires. They fear openness with one another and prefer to socialize little. The gallant youth of the city stay home rather than pursue young women whose beauty and other attractions pale beside the risks of courting them, because their families are considered to possess

2. Facundo's Impact

risky political associations. After eighteen years of regime terrorism, the people of Buenos Aires have modified their natural behavior, subdued their natural inclinations, wiped natural expressions from their faces, and repressed even their hearts' most natural emotions. It is virtually impossible for others to penetrate the protective shell into which each middle-class inhabitant has crawled like a primitive sea creature. The signals that emerge from the shell are often designed to mislead. Outside visitors frequently observe among these inhabitants of the city a sort of false vehemence and repeated, exaggerated expressions of contentment and enthusiasm with no apparent basis in reality.

Letters written by correspondents in Buenos Aires display similar characteristics. The most horrid, irritating, and scandalous sort of thing may occur on a given day, and yet, among a thousand letters written in the city on that day, only one or possibly two will mention it at all. The press is even worse. The man who sits down to read through the last seven years of the local press, comprising hundreds of issues of *La Gazeta*, *El Diario de la Tarde*, and *The British Packet*, will reach, in all cases, the same conclusion, to wit, that the newspapers of Buenos Aires are essentially dead. They publish only words spoken through them, as through a ventriloquist's dummy. Aside from business announcements, their scant coverage deals with the same events, offering the same vapid opinions, in exactly the same words. And even by reading all of them, the curious visitor will get not even the most basic notion of what is really happening in the city. By contrast, today's Chilean press reaches a far-flung readership around the Pacific Ocean from California to Peking, and even those who peruse only an occasional issue of a Chilean newspaper will yet come away with a clear idea of political contests, the forces supporting or opposing various candidates, their background, platforms, virtues, and defects.

Such is the social context within which one must understand the crime of Camila O'Gorman and the panicky reaction in Buenos Aires, less to the crime, per se, than to the "exemplary" punishment meted out by the government of Juan Manuel de Rosas. Camila O'Gorman belonged to a leading family of the city's best society. She was pretty, well-bred, sang and played piano artfully, and lived on a street known for its profusion of stylish boutiques. That last circumstance, in a city where the nightly paseo of elegant young people circles incessantly from shop window to shop window, made her well known among our stylish youth. Her father was more than respectable, a model citizen of refined manners and elegant dress, quite European in his customs, which made him a target for those who, incited by Rosista rabble-rousing, love to hurl mud or oxblood at the wearers of recent European fashion. Recently, even the stylish shaves and haircuts done by certain up-to-date barbers have awakened the brutish persecution of the Rosista constabulary.

Among the visitors who frequented the home of Camila O'Gorman was a young priest, Ladislao Gutiérrez, whose soft-spoken kindness had won him the trust of the entire family. The general climate of secrecy and repression that deforms the social psychology of Buenos Aires sent relations between the young woman and the young cleric down the path of illicit romance and seduction. The result was a shameful pregnancy and the lovers' desperate resolve to escape together into the countryside, where they might have their child and live their sad idyll in anonymity. And that is what they attempted for a short time, wandering from place to place, where Gutiérrez sought employment teaching primary school, until at last they were recognized and their whereabouts revealed to the authorities, who arrested them and transported them in chains back to Buenos Aires, renewing and piquing intense public interest in the case.

At ten o'clock the following morning the regime showed once more its ability to instill fear and public conformity by ordering that all traffic in the streets of Buenos Aires be halted and remain silent to hear an official announcement. Then came the chilling news that Camila O'Gorman, her sacrilegious husband, and their still unborn child had been executed together by order of Governor Rosas, thrown into the same rude wooden box, and buried unceremoniously in the same grave. In a city where people's hearts have been hardened by official terrorism over decades, individual deaths and disappearances have lost much of their former power to horrify. But the extrajudicial killing by firing squad of a wayward cleric, a lovely young woman of good family, and a child that, in the memorable words of the gaucho versifier Ascasubi, "was slaughtered even before he was born"—struck the populace as unexpected and exquisitely horrifying, as if the killing had been done in the street, before their eyes, and the victims' severed heads had been displayed in the marketplace. The people of Buenos Aires contorted collectively, as if receiving an electric shock. I have seen letters that foreign residents of Buenos Aires mailed to correspondents in Chile with extreme expressions of revulsion. Typically, because of the climate of fear and self-censorship already described, these letters failed to say exactly what had occurred.

The mentioned pamphlet provides some heart-wrenching details. The army garrison at Santos Lugares, normally charged with carrying out the government's summary executions, was overwhelmed by the enormity

2. Facundo's Impact

of the orders it received. The officer who received the orders simply refused to obey them, stammering reflexively that he would rather die. Another contingent had to be sent on special orders of the tyrant to form the firing squad. The killers first removed the skin from the palms of Gutierrez's hands and from his scalp, a refinement of cruelty that they had practiced earlier with four other clerics executed at Santos Lugares. Brought out blindfolded and tied into the chair where he was to be shot, the criminal father felt his resolve weaken when he heard more footsteps around him.

"Who is with me?" he asked.

"I am with you," said the voice that had comforted him so often in the past. "And I'm not afraid, so don't you be. They have baptized the child."

Camila threw her head forward so that her hair concealed her face, and when she heard the soldiers of the firing squad cock their weapons, she arched her entire body forward and drew in her belly, as if trying to protect her unborn baby from the bullets. The soldiers of Don Juan Manuel de Rosas are only men of flesh and blood, and when given the order to shoot, one of them passed out as he pulled the trigger. The other seven soldiers turned their faces away when they fired, failing to aim, and when the smoke cleared, not a single bullet had touched either of the blindfolded victims. Ordered to reload and fire again, the soldiers again missed their targets, with the exception of one bullet that grazed the unfortunate señorita's arm, bringing a splatter of blood and a howl of pain. The poor brutes then realized that kindness required they kill without further delay, and their third round left the victims' bodies in tatters.

News like this would have kept half the women of Santiago inside their houses for a week, but Buenos Aires is another matter. Soon afterward the taverns and cafés were filled to overflowing with people speaking about anything and everything except the execution. An occasional trembling, forced laugh conferred an infernal air to their countenances, like Othello's laugh when he suspects the infidelity of Desdemona. Even the next day, persons who made discreet inquiries could still find no one willing to talk. What had happened? The execution of certain dangerous criminals, apparently. That was all.

This is the behavior that my countrymen of Buenos Aires have internalized. When people are afraid that they might be accused of disloyalty to the regime, they go out to socialize in public, showing that they have nothing to hide. When a member of the family rebels against Rosas and gets his throat cut for it, they throw a party to dissociate themselves from the traitor.

2. Facundo's Impact

What could have motivated the regime's brutality toward a young woman and a man of the cloth, both of whom had already disgraced themselves so thoroughly? Could it be a simple, but perhaps understandable, excess of religious zeal? No, because the tolerance of other clerical irregularities by Rosas is well known in Buenos Aires. Intimate gatherings at the tyrant's residence commonly include the concubine of the priest who serves as the tyrant's record-keeping secretary, and off-color jests about it are commonly heard at the gatherings themselves. Those who know the tyrant cite a different motive.

Recent years have seen a notable decline in the rigor with which the regime has enforced its famous mandate and that all who are loyal to it must at all times wear Federalist red to signify their loyalty. Young women of Rosista families began to appear in public without the ribbon. Men's vests, formerly bright red, had gradually darkened to a less Federalist crimson, or even a reddish brown, then black with red pinstripes, finally degenerating to plain black or other colors, with not the slightest admixture of red. Time was, 180 citizens had been jailed on a single occasion for the crime of forgetting to wear anything red. Evidently, the authorities perceived a need to rebuild the dilapidated moral fiber of the citizenry, especially of the youth who had come of age after 1840. Eight years are time enough to forget things, even things so glorious and crucial as the need to wear Federalist red. The foreign surname O'Gorman, the family's social distinction, coupled with its European refinements in customs and dress—these matters, too, appear to have antagonized the regime, suggesting the need for an object lesson. The involvement of a priest and a society girl added notoriety to the lesson taught. And then, news of the European revolutions of 1848 arrived to further roil the waters. The spirit of insubordination is contagious, after all. What more salutary moment for a reminder of who, for whatever motive, can deliver a blow to the heart capable of sending one's spirit and blood flowing away to the extremities for an entire year?

Obras, vol. 6, pp. 207–12

3. *El Chacho*: The Last of a Breed

From an essay on the figure Sarmiento identified as the *last* towering rural leader in Argentina, these short selections reveal a portrait of Angel Vicente "Chacho" Peñaloza that both links him to and distinguishes him from Facundo Quiroga. Written close to two decades after *Facundo*, the story of El Chacho, first published in 1868, allows readers to glimpse how Sarmiento's understanding of the countryside—and the forces necessary to transform it—changed.

Most important for Sarmiento, however, was that El Chacho represented the trailing edge of the ongoing struggle between rural barbarism and urban civilization. Chacho and his gaucho soldiers posed a threat to national unity and had to be defeated. That was exactly what happened under Sarmiento's watch as governor of San Juan and military commander of the Cuyo region. Some of Sarmiento's contemporaries, such as the writers José Hernández (author of the Argentine epic poem *Martín Fierro*) and Olegario Andrade, celebrated the life of El Chacho as the embodiment of an Argentine spirit. Sarmiento saw things in a very different light: in this reflection on "The Last Caudillo of the Llanos," readers will glean a blend of admiration and condemnation. The most salient note is not about Peñaloza himself, but about the future of the country and what stood in the way of achieving that version of the future.

❊ ❊ ❊

3. El Chacho: *The Last of a Breed*

El Chacho, The Last Caudillo of the Llanos

The gaucho montoneras, or mounted guerrillas, who rode with Facundo Quiroga until Quiroga's death later became followers of El Chacho.

El Chacho was another semi-barbarous centaur of the pampas who held sway from the 1840s to the 1860s, wearing gaucho garb and speaking in the extravagant backcountry accent of La Rioja. Chilean observers, immune to the charm of Argentine caudillos, found the rude countryman to have surprising influence over his many more sophisticated fellow officers of urban background. The Argentines found something compelling about El Chacho, despite his many defeats. El Chacho was a taste that Chileans had not acquired, and vice versa. Escaping on one occasion to Chile, El Chacho was asked, "How are you faring, Chacho?" To which he replied "How do you think? In Chile, and on foot!"

There is absolutely nothing worth saying about the man's social origins, except that he was apparently the domestic servant of a priest whose repeated commands to this particular muchacho (chacho, do this; chacho, do that) led to a shortening of his name. An advantage that often goes with serving clergy, the acquisition of literacy, somehow did not accrue to El Chacho. He never learned to read, and as a military commander he merely scratched his mark on orders drafted—and often inspired, too—by whatever scribe or secretary was at hand. That is the normal way with the rural caudillos who have spilled so much blood and exercised such power over the Argentine backlands for so long. The murderous instincts are their own; everything else is the work of whatever scribe or secretary has managed to insinuate himself into the caudillo's confidence.

Blue-eyed, fair of complexion and countenance, almost blond as a boy, El Chacho was easy to look at and difficult to deal with. He wasn't the type to order arbitrary executions out of pure vengefulness, but thousands died because of his thoughtless uprisings. He did not seek personal enrichment, and his wife was a woman of worthy character and intelligence, but El Chacho studiously resisted acquiring those traits.

Even when his public life put him in contact with worthy, cultivated people, he remained raw and brutish. He intentionally retained and also exaggerated the rustic way of speaking that one hears in the Argentine far west, where Spanish has been spoken without adequate civilized models for two centuries. El Chacho spoke in a manner calculated to communicate his cultural affinity with the least sophisticated among his gaucho followers. If his civilized critics found him grotesque, it only made him

3. El Chacho: *The Last of a Breed*

more memorable. He always lived in a hut of mud-daub construction and thatched roof, just like any humble gaucho, although in later years he had a proper bedroom constructed to offer to overnight visitors from the city. He commonly lounged around the hut in his poncho and underclothes, with a kerchief tied around his head, drinking mate. Like many of our gauchos, he considered long underwear the height of fashion, and he sometimes hiked up his uniform trousers to display his clean white undergarment. He doubled down on any behavior that seemed outrageous to those with more civilized tastes, never conveying a full spoon to his mouth, for example, without dribbling onto the tablecloth, even when a guest of the most punctilious hostess. During the last years of his life, El Chacho drank heavily. In fact, when not terrifying the countryside with his reckless violence or attending horse races, which periodically draw contenders and spectators across a wide swath of the plains for several days, he spent almost all his time on a bench in the shade, smoking and drinking either alcohol or yerba mate.

The difference between mine and thine is sometimes not so clear out on the pampas, and even less so when El Chacho's guerrilla raiders entered the streets of a town, expecting all sorts of tributes, gifts, and myriad forms of material collaboration. For example, the followers of El Chacho had dedicated themselves, one fine day, to looting and burning everything in my native land of San Juan when another officer, a man planning a future presidential bid (our friend Derquí, in fact), gave the order that looters would be executed.[1] Five looters were apprehended red-handed, but El Chacho stepped in and had them all released in recognition of their faithful services. Likewise, El Chacho patiently indulged whatever minor murders and throat-cuttings his men might accidentally commit in the process of imposing order. When not engaged in a larger conflict, El Chacho served as a sort of freelance enforcer within the Argentine Republic, taking one side or another of whatever local conflict presented an opportunity for his involvement. In this way he served a string of masters over the years, including Quiroga, Lavalle, and Rosas himself; Urquiza and Mitre too. On four occasions, alleging this or that, he made a show of force by riding with his gauchos into San Juan. He did the same three times in Tucumán, once in San Luis, once in Córdoba. One is reminded of the way desert Arabs in North Africa provide military services to established governments while preserving tribal autonomy.

---

1. Santiago Derquí was president of Argentina for a very short period (1860–1861).

3. El Chacho: *The Last of a Breed*

How did this anomalous barbarism last decades in the Argentine Republic? El Chacho was not particularly efficacious in a fight. In fact, I could find no reference to a skirmish in which El Chacho actually triumphed. Oddly, however, this circumstance failed to diminish the intense hold he exercised over his followers. Why?

El Chacho's followers willingly faced privations and even death at his command. His many small defeats bled his followers grievously. Among gaucho guerrillas, to be well-mounted means to escape a defeat, while to be poorly mounted means to be lanced from behind by victorious pursuers. El Chacho's ragtag guerrillas were always poorly mounted. For the same reason, rarely did an unwounded man try to evacuate a wounded comrade. Two men on one horse would surely not escape, so the wounded got left behind. The mentality of these men corresponds to their desert environment, just as occurs in Arab countries. The starkness of the desert shapes their sensibility. Because of their limited contact with civilization, they are easily dazzled by wine, delicacies, fine horses and apparel. They desire to enjoy such luxuries and will fight to retain them. Strong new stimuli disorient them, but unlike educated people, they lack the habit of reflection and therefore cannot process the personal meaning of such transformations. Deep atavistic forces unify them under the guidance of someone like El Chacho.

This atavism derives not only from isolation and ignorance, but also from Indigenous tradition. They seem not to learn from their mistakes, nor, left unpunished, do they ever change their ways. They engage the enemy on impulse, without calculating the odds, then flee from battle as soon as they perceive the slightest disadvantage therein. Gaucho warfare is not a decisive interruption of life, but rather a constituent part of it, an activity wherein the group constitutes and recognizes itself. Facundo Quiroga stirred the atavistic impulses among them beginning in 1825. Thereafter, Quiroga was able to whistle up his armed retainers repeatedly. Pretty much all men and boys of military age responded to his call, reproducing in America the social organization of Asian pastoral nomads since time immemorial. The habits of command and obedience are transmitted from father to son until they become second nature. El Chacho inherited the atavism unleashed by Quiroga, and therefore he never had to make use of conscription or the other forms of coercion required by the military establishments of civilized nations. After all, his prospective followers had little to gain by refusing his call to arms. Their miserable huts were scenes more of protracted hunger than domestic bliss, whereas war promised a little excitement, at least, possibly some kind of reward,

3. El Chacho: *The Last of a Breed*

surely new vistas, a ride on a railroad train, the chance to perform one's masculinity and recuperate the feeling of being alive.

This impressive group solidarity apparently derives from an Indigenous substrate, in this case, stemming from the Guaraní-speaking populations of Entre Ríos, Corrientes, and Paraguay. One also sees this spontaneous group response among the Quechua-speaking populations of the Province of Santiago del Estero, where the good sense of those to whom the group responds have made it a bastion of state power, rather than a loose cannon. This sort of solidarity explains the irrepressible montoneras that responded to the call of El Chacho Peñaloza, despite his many and multifaceted defeats. This was the power base of backcountry caudillos like him—something atavistic, patriarchal, rooted in Indigenous traditions. This was the phenomenon, too, that impeded the creation of modern government in the Argentine Republic until 1862. The rule of law—with its schools, legislatures, judges, and enlightened citizenry—had to wait for thirty years while rural satraps like El Chacho Peñalosa reigned supreme.

Or, semi-supreme. Consider the challenges that Peñalosa faced in his mid-sixties, when his astonishing ability to vanish and escape undetected across unimaginable distances had not ceased to impress—without, however, fully concealing an inconvenient truth. Escapes were El Chacho's only victories. When cornered and forced to fight, he usually lost. And while he always escaped personally, many of his followers—dozens, adding up to hundreds—did not.

Given this inconvenient truth, some of the old lion's followers naturally harkened to the prideful vigor of younger war captains. Perhaps old Nestor must make way for young Achilles? Irrazábal was married among the Pampas Indians, it was said, and that kind of alliance with savage tribes confers prestige in our rural milieu. Los Saa was another clan that owed its ascendancy on the pampas to the sort of activities captained over the years by El Chacho. One Saa member even got to be a brigadier general of the Argentine Confederation. Then there was Ontivero, a great friend of other men's property, who believed that all prisoners' throats should be ventilated, as in the good old days of Rosas.

Here, then, was the opposition to old Nestor.

Ontivero, believing the time to be right, went to the hut that El Chacho used as his headquarters, waving a revolver, challenging El Chacho's leadership, and threatening to leave the montonera. El Chacho refused to be intimidated, and he thoroughly outtalked the younger man, throwing in his face his violent extortions of the rural population, violent extortions

3. El Chacho: The Last of a Breed

that were ruining the montonera's reputation. Ontivero took whatever he wanted by force of arms, and that's the way it should be, he said openly. Hadn't Facundo Quiroga mobilized a lot of resources that way? Spectators tell how El Chacho launched one of his famous putdowns at this moment. "If you're so brave," he said to Ontivero, "then why did you run away that day at Punta del Agua? And why don't you go toss out the judge of San Juan? Or better yet, why don't you go after Colonel Arredondo? Why *don't* you?"

At bottom, though, old Nestor was shaken to find his orders questioned and his patriarchal authority challenged for the first time. Even as he ridiculed the challenge mounted by the analogues of Achilles, El Chacho sidled in the direction of his horse and, reaching it, clambered onto the animal's back in the undignified manner that gauchos consider to be no shame at all, saying that he could see when he wasn't wanted and that he had no wish to impose himself on people who lacked the natural good taste to prefer his company. Then he rode calmly away from the camp of the montonera, apparently in no hurry, arriving home a few days later. Much as San Martín did, you might observe, following his famous meeting with Bolívar.

El Chacho's theatrical gesture had the desired effect. The shouting match had attracted attention, and word of El Chacho's departure moved quickly through the montonera. Why, after all, had Ontivero run away at Punta del Agua? For that reason, or perhaps out of blind loyalty, El Chacho's men began to pack their bags and saddle their horses, and then, one after another, to follow the lone figure of their caudillo away from the camp. The exodus became general. Ontivero found himself alone with his cluster of devoted rascals. Eventually he had to apologize, which he did with enough apparent sincerity that El Chacho forgave him and the montonera's crisis of leadership was overcome.

Ontivero had reason to fear Colonel Arredondo. Arredondo eventually caught up with El Chacho's montonera, and neither Ontivero nor El Chacho survived their meeting. The montonera had escaped a close scrape and gotten away, apparently, at least. El Chacho put three mountain ridges between the montonera and Arredondo's pursuers, but he didn't get away. He made it as far as an isolated village called Olta, where he normally considered himself safe. Not this time. El Chacho's first indication of disaster was when he looked up and saw Arredondo's soldiers

3. El Chacho: *The Last of a Breed*

surrounding him. A few of his lieutenants escaped, but El Chacho simply surrendered.

Olta is normally secure because outsiders approaching the village may be observed an hour before they arrive. On that day, however, there was a rain shower that allowed fifty men of Arredondo's advance party to approach without warning. El Chacho was resting, meditating on his next move, no doubt. But he never made a next move. The commander of Arredondo's advance party identified El Chacho, executed him, and placed his head on a pike in the dusty center of Olta for a week, following the practice normally applied to bandits and horse thieves on the pampa.

Ontivero's end came a bit later, somewhat south of San Luis, when he appeared with a bunch of renegade Indians outside Fort Mercedes, trying as always to parlay the situation to his advantage. Ontivero approached the fort to examine its defenses, but he went too close or moved too slowly. One of the defenders, said to be a Frenchman, hit Ontivero in the forehead with a lucky long shot, which of course was the end of him. The Indians took one look at his lifeless body and went home.

And so ended, for all time, the career of the sadly famous montonera created by Facundo Quiroga in 1826. If Argentina is not yet finished with civil wars, at least we can expect no more uprisings of gauchos and Indians on these lonely plains that have suffered so long and endured so much. The railroad will transform the pampa rapidly, no doubt, and the rustic protagonists of frontier life will disappear here, just as they have disappeared from the North American frontier described by James Fenimore Cooper. Figures like El Chacho and Ontivero, while undeniably real, will seem as remote and inexplicable as the dinosaur bones recently unearthed on the pampa. This, rather than any individual life or death, is the importance of what happened at Olta in 1863.

The death of El Chacho Peñalosa closed the long cycle of montonera uprisings begun by Artigas and Quiroga decades earlier. The montoneras of Artigas doomed Spanish colonialism on our shores, while the montoneras of Quiroga long delayed efforts to create a unified Argentine Republic in its place. Only the railroad, crisscrossing the pampa with steel rails, can ensure that the montoneras never ride again.

Obras, vol. 7, pp. 280–84; 352–53; 360–61, 374

4. Immigration and the Expanding Frontier

"To govern is to populate," wrote Juan Bautista Alberdi, one of Sarmiento's contemporaries. Attracting immigrants—though not just any immigrants—to fill the vast countryside and expand the frontier became a political imperative in Argentina in the second half of the 1800s. Sarmiento dreamed of Northern Europeans bringing their civilized ways to correct Argentine faults. But the story played out very differently than he had hoped, as we see through his shifting views on immigration and the roles immigrants should have in Argentine society.

❊ ❊ ❊

"Immigration,"
in *El Nacional*, 25 July 1855

It has been calculated that during the final years of the Rosas regime, about six thousand European immigrants a year were arriving in Buenos Aires. And yet, during that period, no extraordinary new commercial activity revealed the presence of immigrants. Possibly ten thousand more have entered during the last two years, and yet salaries remain steady at twenty pesos a day, and twice that for workers with significant experience in the manual arts. Some earn more yet.

Just imagine the cost of labor in Argentina without those thirty thousand additional immigrants of recent years. How many thousands more may arrive without depressing wages one iota! High-quality European

4. Immigration and the Expanding Frontier

immigration produces optimal results such as those visible in the United States. There, steadily increasing immigration has resulted over half a century in an average wage that has slipped, only very recently, below a dollar a day. The other half of the cost of labor is the high price of basic foodstuffs and all sorts of daily necessities, because that's where much of the laborers' money goes. The surprising prosperity of the United States derives from the constant juxtaposition of those two factors: high salaries and a low cost of living. The US worker can buy three times as much with his salary when compared with Argentine workers earning a comparable wage. They use it to buy three times the food, three times the living space, three times the clothing, three times everything more than Argentine workers. And sometimes those workers buy their own little piece of land or accumulate their own little capital and begin a new productive activity that will require more workers and justify higher salaries.

Consider the example of New York City, with about half a million inhabitants and, like Buenos Aires, emporium and entrepôt for a vast commercial hinterland. New York is the port of entry for thousands of immigrants, and its harbor on the Hudson welcomes the largest number of seagoing vessels in the Americas. In the whole world, only the Thames floats more international bottoms. When those ships set sail for myriad ports of call around the world, their holds are full of provisions for their lengthy voyages, some of those provisions carefully packed in ice. The abundance and low cost of provisions in New York City has kept salaries at a reasonable level in spite of the tremendous demand for laborers, including those needed to crew the hundreds of whaling vessels that put to sea annually. A hundred thousand square miles of cultivated land and seven railroad lines, measuring together three thousand five hundred miles, work together to supply the city, not to mention canals, navigable rivers, and Long Island Sound.

To speak here in Buenos Aires about the advantages of immigration is to rain, as they say, on what's already wet. In Buenos Aires, we feel the advantages of immigration all around us, every day. Everyone talks about how to encourage it. Recent statistics suggest that, if one deducts the number of emigrants that left the country last year, the net gain was only four thousand five hundred immigrants, less than fifty thousand in ten years. This is a paltry figure when compared with the current needs of Argentina, which could put that many new laborers to work in a single year.

The Buenos Aires office of statistics is hobbled now, as ever, by the negligence of all the minor officials whose job it is to report the raw

4. Immigration and the Expanding Frontier

information, yet its reports merit our attention when considering immigration. Demographic information suggests that women outnumbered men, among rural people in the past generation, because of the death tolls produced by our decades of civil war. At present, however, the tables seem to have been turned, owing to the large predominance of males among the immigrants now arriving in Argentina. To believe our statistical publications, about one third more women are needed to achieve a gender balance. This disequilibrium of population cannot but contribute to a general disorganization of family life that is observable today. I have figures here from the countryside, no need to say exactly where, in which no fewer than 174 out of 281 infants were born out of wedlock. Many of their parents simply lacked a word from the kindly curate, prodding them to regularize their union in the eyes of God. The absence of clergy in too many of our rural parishes contributes not a little to perpetuate moral laxity.

In France there are fewer marriages than in Buenos Aires, even though France has civil, as well as religious, authorities, empowered to marry people. In New York, there is one wedding a year for every seventy inhabitants, twice as many per capita as in France or Buenos Aires, and in Boston they marry yet more often. A high rate of marriage suggests the overall health of US society, the educational attainments of the people at large, the vibrancy of the economy, and very especially, the facility of acquiring land, whether public or available at low prices along the frontier of colonization.

The foundation of a marriage is the house and property that give it security. In order to lead productive lives, working families will need a basis such as that. In enlightened lands, legislators provide lands for future generations. Imagine the bizarre practice of exercising foresight in such a matter, rather than turning over territory to the highest bidder. Imagine that a boy studies from four to fourteen, learns a trade, marries at the age of twenty or so, and then simply moves to the place where lots have been made available.

No such dream scenarios occur in Argentina, yet the Buenos Aires office of statistics provides pertinent data. Immigrants here marry more often than native-born people. In the suburban zone of Barracas del Sud, with just shy of five thousand inhabitants, about half the men who married were immigrants. We also have information on 130 marriages in which 77 of the grooms were immigrants, far over-representing their proportion of the population. In this group, no fewer than 26 young native-born women were marrying immigrants. Meanwhile, the tiny proportion

4. Immigration and the Expanding Frontier

of Protestant residents from northern European countries accounted for one twentieth of the weddings in the second half of 1854, as well as 60 births, every one of them legitimate.

Immigration plays an important role in Argentina. Immigrants are contributing powerfully to the recovery of family life, undermined by extensive livestock raising generally, but threatened particularly, during recent decades, by the decimation of our rural male population. In a country needful of population, the immigrants procreate more rapidly, by all indications, than does the native-born population. Immigrant men seem to marry three times more often than their native-born counterparts. This is not unusual. In the United States, immigrant women actually bear more children than do native-born women.

Let's look at just a few more statistics. Where are those missing native-born grooms? In the rural areas around Buenos Aires, eighteen thousand Argentine men are day laborers, real gauchos, normally itinerant, without a family, often without a roof over their heads. More than two thousand natives appear classified as unemployed vagrants, almost certainly an undercount, whereas only fifty foreigners found themselves unemployed at the moment of the census. Immigrants are, above all, the necessary counterbalance to a backward and unproductive element of our rural population, one that contributes in no small measure to our constant state of civil alarm.

Let us take a lesson from the Vendée region of France, which, in the late 1700s, somewhat resembled Argentina, with its predominance of traditional herders and its feudal labor relations. The Vendée region, infested by a thousand religious fanatics, scuttled the revolutionary transformations of the first French Republic. Napoleon knew what to do about it. He opened the region up with a great road, from one side to the other, to clear away the fog of backwardness. After that the inhabitants lost interest in destructive crusades of all kinds. And a different kind of road, a railroad, would work the same sort of magic here. Railroads are what we need so that immigrants can fan out, so that producers can work wherever they find the materials, throughout the national territory, confident that their link to the international market is easy, inexpensive, safe, and fast. Immigrant enterprise starts small, a few extra hens for an egg business, a milk cow. The railroad is the essential infrastructural support for that kind of small-time economic enterprise in the countryside.

Obras, vol. 23, pp. 358–63

"Organized Settlement Projects," in *El Nacional*, 8 August 1878

Buenos Aires Province, where public land is unavailable, offers little incentive to the potential organizers of settlement projects. Land in Buenos Aires Province is divided into large estancias and controlled by the owners of those estancias, who show slight inclination to sell it. Around pampean towns there is cropland, of course, and fenced areas for crop cultivation are appearing on more estancias these days. While these situations offer opportunities to immigrant agricultural laborers, they generally do not offer any avenue to landowning, which is what immigrants want and what settlement is all about.

Buenos Aires and our other cities provide employment for many artisans and workers, but given that new ones arrive daily, there is a need for rapid turnover. Many circumstances can slow the overall process, including external conditions over which we have no control, such as a temporary financial crisis in Europe or a drop in the price of our export products in European markets. Only the availability of land for the arriving immigrants can assure their permanent settlement and build the population base in the localities that welcome them.

More than merely being available at a reasonable cost, in order to favor the arrival of settlers land must be located near the sort of market that can absorb the small-scale production of perishables like eggs or milk that immigrant farmers have for sale in the first few years after their arrival, before the large-scale production of exportable crops can begin. One can hardly describe that arrival of the Swiss in Baradero as a state-organized settlement project, but its evident success derives precisely from the arrangement that I have just described. Each arriving family received only a small plot of land, but the advantages of the location near the urban market of Buenos Aires allowed the incoming families to earn money steadily in the first ten years and subsequently expand their landholdings and establish themselves on a firm basis, whether near the site of their first arrival, or by selling their original property and buying a larger extension in another location.

The settlement project of the Province of Santa Fe, on which we want to focus this discussion, has many advantages, but its relationship to major communications infrastructure leaves much to be desired. Many of the zones scheduled for settlement lie a great distance from Rosario, the only deepwater port in the region, where large vessels load entire crops at an expensive going rate. One house of the legislature has already

4. Immigration and the Expanding Frontier

approved a project for an up-to-date narrow-gauge railway that, at a cost of three thousand pounds sterling per mile, will connect a number of settlements. Others are already growing together along the route, offering a continuous vista of plowed landscape or bristling fields of grain for mile after mile, studded occasionally with the mills necessary to convert all that grain into flour. If the project becomes a reality, the Province of Santa Fe will boast the leading example of large-scale organized settlement in all South America.

Now is the time for us to move forward with other measures designed to foment immigration. Responsible, well-established immigrant settlers should be allowed to request new immigrants from the same locale of origin in Europe and advance the cost of their transatlantic passage. All that is required additionally is legislation to formalize the new immigrants' responsibility to repay the debt they owe the man who paid their tickets in advance. This measure will help address the need for existing settlements to intensify their production within their present limits. With most of their land area already plowed, existing settlements cannot absorb many more full-salaried workers, but there is still need for the kind of supporting and associated population, including younger and older people of both sexes, such as elderly aunts and uncles, who will play their economic roles on a voluntary basis and who normally become involved in small-scale agricultural activities part-time as part of a larger family effort.

These are exactly the sort of people who are most likely to be recruited to immigrate by others already well-established. These are the sort of new arrivals who will help fill in the gaps between already existing settlements, populating the interstices with both producers and consumers. In that manner, the viability of the railroad is assured by the density of economic activity along its tracks. Anyone interested in the overall success of Argentina's organized settlement projects, of course including the national government, ought to pay attention to this matter, because the continuation and future growth of our present immigration depends on the outcome of our current efforts in the Province of Santa Fe. What could be a more desirable outcome than the creation of a vast, well-populated expanse of cropland, punctuated at intervals by towns of proportional size, bound together by inexpensive rail transportation, offering opportunities for market access on every side?

Market access, the facility of importation and exportation, is the key to success here. Subsistence agriculture, the activities by which people seek merely to supply themselves with life's necessities without producing

4. Immigration and the Expanding Frontier

anything for sale, is the path that our rural people have followed traditionally, and it leads to mediocrity and poverty. The fruits of rural labor in our country must be priced competitively so as to enter foreign markets and maintain themselves against foreign products at home. The various improvements that I have been discussing will all tend to reduce the cost of our local products and eliminate the situation whereby the cost of carting a ton of wheat flour to the dock in Buenos Aires is as much as the cost of shipping it to England. Labor, on the other hand, must remain relatively expensive for the foreseeable future, given that advantageous salaries, when combined with a modest cost of living, must constitute the primary attraction for further immigrants. Gradually, however, the price of labor will also rise, when sufficiently compensated by other advantages. That is the case now in the United States, where the recent upward trend in salaries has not slowed economic growth, thanks to the continued low cost of land, many improvements in transportation infrastructure, and the most advanced technologies of production in a national market that now encompasses forty-four million.

To conclude these remarks, let us note a final virtue possessed by the Province of Santa Fe, as well as by some others in the same general part of the country: the quality of the soil. We have reviewed the many economic advantages possessed by the United States, but we must note that it cannot compete with Santa Fe regarding the quality of soils available for plowing. Most of the eastern United States was densely forested when the time came to clear the land for agriculture. Felling and removing the trees is a small job when compared with removal of all the stumps, an enormously labor-intensive task prior to the completion of which no plowing can occur. Such situations are not uncommon in areas of the world currently available for integration into the international market. In Brazil, for example, the climate is such that six months after cutting its dense cover of tropical forest, would-be farmers find a new covering of tough roots and sprouts. In contrast, the alluvial soils of Santa Fe and other provinces of the riverine northeast might seem to have been expressly prepared by Mother Nature, stripped of troublesome rock for the unobstructed operations of an English steam plow. The ready-to-plow character of new ground in areas of Argentina suitable for organized settlement constitutes an inestimable boon to the prospective settler who had contemplated putting in a first crop without major expenditures of capital or labor. Once the few bushes and carob trees have been removed, a steady supply of firewood can be maintained by planting peach trees for fruit and fuel.

In conclusion, let me not create a misleading vision of paradise. Let us remember that challenges still remain. There have been a number of destructive droughts and also locust infestations in recent years, although the excessive rains of the present moment have made each of those problems fade quickly from memory. There is no reason and no time for overconfidence. We must devote ourselves to perfecting what is already good in our existing planned settlements if we want to assure that the stream of agricultural settlers will continue to arrive on our shores well into the future. To accomplish that, I have recommended that we encourage well-established immigrants to invite others from their European places of origin to join them in Argentina. Many advantages are to be gained by filling in the cracks between existing settlements with a dense and multifaceted secondary stream of socially integrated, invited immigrants who will supply minor subsistence products at reasonable prices to the high-salaried workers who produce our exportable surplus of wheat.

Obras, vol. 41, pp. 40–45

"The Indians,"
in *El Nacional*, 2 November 1879

Multiple concerns have clouded our collective horizons of late, but news from our southern frontier, at least, is encouraging. If only all our current affairs could turn out so well!

For a year now the Indians have felt the sharp steel of our valiant men-at-arms, and our southern plains no longer constitute a refuge where the savages can escape military discipline in the future. Our soldiers are battling renegade chieftains in a theater many hundreds of miles in extension. We hear of a victory over Pincen, Catriel, or Namuncurá, then of another over the Ranqueles, as our soldiers go beyond merely defending our frontiers to proactively destroy the Indian encampments in distant hideaways, erase all trace of them, and deposit the miserable survivors in Christian towns.

The early successes of this operation will greatly favor the minister of war's overall effort to deal with the lingering problems of our southern frontier. Whenever that effort is concluded, one can affirm that the

4. Immigration and the Expanding Frontier

groundwork has already been laid. Our strong blows have forced the savages to abandon territories that they have long inhabited. The staggering material losses that they suffered during the present campaign will be even more sorely felt with the demoralizing loss of their homeland, because, make no mistake, the Indians adore their pastures and hunting grounds no less than Greenlanders adore their seals and glaciers. For primitive peoples, the loss of their natural habitat is more grievous than it is for civilized nations. They will not be able to reconstruct as good a life in their new homeland, once established, for many long years. In his celebrated novels, the author James Fenimore Cooper has evoked the desolation and ultimate disintegration of similarly displaced Indigenous tribes in North America.

The definitive solution of our southern Indian problems, begun by Alsina, now to be concluded by Roca, gained momentum gradually over a number of years. It is difficult now to explain just why our military forces seemed so ineffectual twenty years ago, the degree to which we seemed to have lost confidence that modern troops could triumph over Indian lancers, how Indian braves were able to approach and lance our infantry soldiers as they stood in formation, why a contingent of breastplated cuirassiers concealed themselves in a corral where they trembled and begged for mercy, or why, on one famous occasion, our forces sneaked away under cover of darkness rather than face the warriors of Calfurucá. For a long time, settlers on our southern frontier did not dare to take the slightest actions against the savages without support from the army. Fortunately, the immoderate fear of twenty years ago dissipated because of the various defeats eventually suffered by Calfurucá, who lost his ability to terrorize peaceful frontier settlements, except for an occasional raid to carry away this or that herd of semi-wild horses. If not for the continued incitement to rebellion and civil war of various forces stationed on the frontier, and if not for the eight hundred braves brought to the frontier by the chieftain Cartel, our southern pampas would long since have been pacified. Half of the expenses incurred by our military in recent years have been spent to recapture renegade groups that had already been pacified once but, with our loss of military momentum, left the places where we had resettled them and went back to menacing the frontier. The clearest demonstration of progress is the new spirit of our settlers in southern Buenos Aires or Mendoza, who now mobilize of their own accord to defend themselves against Indian raiders and then to pursue and punish them for their insolent misbehavior, without waiting for the army. Thanks to this new élan of our men-at-arms, whether militia or regular army, we have now pacified a huge swath of open plains reaching from southern Buenos Aires to northern Santa Fe.

As General Roca has demonstrated, the most significant new development of our long struggle against the savages is not the decimation of their fighting strength but, rather, our new ability to strike them in their encampments on their home ground. As recently as ten years ago, that would have been an act of madness. It was necessary that the protective frontier between settlement and Indian territory be consolidated under Gainza, and that it advance under Alsina, before Roca could carry the fight against Indian encampments on their home ground.

Now, whether or not we occupy the Río Negro as the natural consequence of our military sweep to the south, we will be able to diminish the size of our deployment within a few years, because the savages will need many years to absorb the blows that we have struck against them already. They seem, at this point, truly doomed. Savages can rarely recover from losses that they suffer by entering in contact with civilized societies. In such encounters, our Indians, like all other savages remaining in the modern world, are on the wrong side of history, condemned to ultimate extinction.

So, just imagine! What is each motley group of defeated individuals that the army rounds up and escorts away from the frontier? Another backward tribe disappearing from the face of the earth, neither more nor less!

Obras, vol. 41, pp. 282–84

"The Campaign against the Indians," in *El Nacional*, 22 February 1879

Readers of this column will remember how, not long ago, I suggested the utility of arranging in chronological order the field reports submitted by the commanders of our valiant military in their long struggle against the savage tribes of the southern frontier. The collection of such documents would bring an enormous number of separate expeditions into view, each with its own leader-protagonists, its own complement of bit players, its own Indigenous antagonists. Happily, at least one veteran officer has seen fit to respond, and his notes jotted "on the fly" in the precious moments of rest between skirmishes furnish the basis of the following chronology

4. Immigration and the Expanding Frontier

of operations against the savages conducted between 1875 and 1878. There's also more recent news of Freire's brilliant expedition into Indian hideouts at the headwaters of the Colorado River.

One period, including perhaps twenty engagements fought by the southern division, can properly be termed the Alsina period, for it is Alsina who began the reorientation of our military forces and began to concentrate them in the southwestern quadrant of Buenos Aires Province. Next, the completion and complement of Alsina's vision, embracing all our frontiers to the south and west of the Argentine Republic and blazing the trail toward our ultimate occupation of the Río Negro, can properly be termed the Roca period. Preceding these two was the Gainza period, which laid the foundations for what came later. It was under Gainza that the republic reclaimed valuable territories from the savages in the provinces of Córdoba and Santa Fe, while in southern Buenos Aires Province we completed a line of forts to serve as bastions and, crucially, telegraph stations where news of Indian incursions could be gathered and promptly relayed to trigger the deployment of major military forces.

That was a turning point. Until that time, the savages dominated the southern pampa of Buenos Aires both morally and militarily. Calfurucá was able to throw his weight around because he commanded two thousand braves. Two thousand well-mounted savage lancers kept the forces of civilization at bay. Well do I remember that, at the beginning of the Sarmiento administration, absolutely everything remained to be done. Our involvement in the Paraguayan war had siphoned away all the state's frontier resources, military and otherwise, and that opened us to deadly raiding by the Indians on a regular basis. My administration quickly improvised defensive measures, stationing contingents of troops outside frontier towns and reducing the size of raiding parties to renegade groups of a few braves.

We succeeded in putting so much pressure on the savages that Calfurucá organized a defensive league of Indian chieftains. His goal was to destroy the line of forts that we had established along our southern frontier, to deal us such a blow as to return the state of affairs to the Indian predominance that had existed at the time when my administration took charge. The gigantic raid organized by Calfurucá temporarily disrupted our fortifications and communications, not to mention the booty that his followers managed to extract from the herds of Christian settlers, reportedly sixty thousand cattle and a proportionate number of horses. Fortunately, he could not escape our valiant forces under General Rivas, who defeated Calfurucá, actually unhorsed him as well as many of his braves. Those who managed to return to their encampments did so on foot or mounted comically three

4. Immigration and the Expanding Frontier

to a horse. Calfurucá might have been annihilated then and there, had General Rivas been able fully to implement my orders. Be that as it may, Calfurucá's defeat on that occasion broke the military power of the savages, who ceased their destructive raiding into lands occupied by our settlers. Within a year, control of areas where the natives encamped seemed to be within reach. One of our interminable civil conflicts erupted at that point. The élan and momentum of our frontier forces was lost as the savages became aware of our internal weakness. The chieftain Catriel, at the head of eight hundred lancers, no longer accepted pacification and abandoned his agreement to cooperate with the army. When his seasoned fighters switched sides, the insecurity of the frontier became the worst of any time since 1868.

That was the situation encountered by Alsina, who then assumed his responsibilities as minister of war. It has often been noted that the savages are keenly aware of the weakness and disorganization created by our civil wars. Catriel's people had chosen the timing of several previous uprisings to coincide with partisan fighting among Christians. The overthrow of Rosas and the subsequent skirmishes gave them one such excuse. The new minister of war approached the campaign with vigor, not limiting himself to restoration of the frontier line of forts, but rather taking the war to the savages' home ground.

This systematic change in strategy is entirely to his credit and will redound to his everlasting glory.

Namuncurá, the son of Calfurucá, and other chieftains now faced the bullets of our advanced forces in their home encampments. Whatever strange enchantment had bewitched our fighting men disappeared entirely with the realization that the Indians' home encampments were neither inaccessible nor impregnable. Various chieftains and their people were scattered about, here and there, in contrast to the united front they made when raiding our settlers. To be on the offensive had been the Indians' entire strategy. Under attack on their home ground, they proved unable to mount a vigorous defense. They did not lack bravery, but they had lost the spirit of victory, never to regain it.

On his deathbed, Alsina continued the great work, directing its advancement with his last strength. Much remained to be done, as he saw clearly, and he was able pass the project, finally, into hands as committed and competent as his own. May he rest in peace.

With that, let us pass to turn to the information I mentioned at the outset. The notes that I append below have been graciously provided to me by a veteran officer, responding to my plea for information:

Southeastern Frontier

The following events took place on the southeastern frontier during the wars against the savage from the year 1875 to the year 1878.

Much has been written about the Indians of the Pampas during more than three centuries.

Our leaders believed that the slow advance of settlement would eliminate the Indian problem, but that did not occur.

It fell to the illustrious Dr. Adolfo Alsina to deal with the problem adequately.

The savage employs tactics quite different from those that compose the modern arts of civilized warfare. The savage is a nomadic wanderer who never tills the soil and does not know the meaning of honest labor. To the contrary, he tries to live entirely by his wits, much preferring to steal anything that he should require. The savage does not lack bravery, and on occasion he has been known to gallop into a formation of regular line troops armed only with his lance.

Nonetheless, his normal procedure is to flee from combat in the most cowardly manner. The savage will only fight to hold on to stolen goods or when he finds himself strong numerically.

Only men with special knowledge of the savage, of his habits and his reactions, can fight him successfully.

The savage attacks in a dispersed formation, shouting infernally.

He relies totally on the initial shock of his attack to defeat us, and if his first charge does not do so, he retreats immediately out of range of our Remingtons to plot another treacherous attack from a different angle. . . .

Obras, vol. 41, pp. 310–13

"Naturalizing the Millions,"
in *El Diario*, 16 November 1887

Day before yesterday saw the publication of an initiative, signed by Antonio Cambaceres, formerly director of the board of elections, promoting the naturalization of foreign-born persons who have immigrated to the Argentine Republic. The proposed law would confer citizenship

4. Immigration and the Expanding Frontier

on said persons automatically, "without their having requested it," on the grounds that requesting citizenship is a personal embarrassment.

That is the gist of the initiative, which has already garnered a number of respectable signatures, including those appended to an earlier version. A name which figured formerly in favor, and appeared at the special urging of the original organizers, but has been withdrawn from the current proposal—is that of yours truly. Simply put, I cannot support a law treating citizenship in the Argentine Republic as a personal embarrassment. My reasoning on the matter has been explained in the public forum. A distinction must be made between those who have truly immigrated and those whose presence in Argentina is accidental or temporary. Surely none would argue that the rights of citizenship ought to accrue to temporary residents whose true domicile remains in their countries of origin. Does one earn the right to govern us simply by setting foot on our shores?

To the many who have sought my opinion regarding whether or not to support the initiative themselves, let me be clear. I advise against it. It would be an unprecedented misstep, an untried notion certain to produce an undesired result. The idea flies in the face of human history. Did not the ancient Athenians refuse to concede citizenship in Athens even to other Greeks? To begin, numerous practical difficulties would arise, as a result, in our relations with various European nations. England refuses to allow the principle of dual citizenship, for example, and France declines to grant foreign nationals equal status before the law. Only the countries of North and South America immediately grant to immigrants the same civil rights that are enjoyed by their natural-born citizens.

Some rights correspond to all urban residents, of whatever nationality, by virtue of their residence. They walk the streets, live in the houses, use the water. They form the population and must participate in managing its collective affairs. Something different are the political rights that confer the faculty of governance. Upon taking up residence in any country in North or South America, immigrants with foreign citizenship (or no citizenship at all) may join a new political community unconditionally. All they must do is inform the proper authority of their will to assume the new responsibilities and privileges. Their free will is of the essence, the will to exercise the rights that they thereby formally request. Where, without that request, is their will expressed?

The natural-born citizen indicates his political rights by displaying record of his local baptism. The naturalized citizen indicates his by displaying the record of his lawful immigration and the signed declaration of his will to acquire citizenship. Citizenship comprises responsibilities

4. Immigration and the Expanding Frontier

as well as privileges. By what sign will the new arrival have indicated his acceptance of those responsibilities? Can anyone who comes to this country and stays two years take a hand in governing it?

The logical weakness of the current initiative is everywhere evident. What are we to make of a petition signed by foreign nationals, formally requesting that they be granted citizenship without requesting it? And logic matters when the prize is the power of governance. Imagine half a million immigrants requesting unrequested citizenship as soon as they have become the majority: it would amount to a peaceful coup d'état. The power to govern, when exercised by a majority, is the power to rule. And such ideas are already being floated in Buenos Aires and Santa Fe.

This would matter less if the initiative under consideration did not betray the authors' complete inexperience in dealing with immigration matters, whose conventional wisdom recommends that citizenship not be offered to new arrivals before a period of time has elapsed. To contemplate making citizenship automatic is already too much; to contemplate making that change permanent and irreversible is outrageous, and that is what is now being proposed to the Congress. The United States has already taken in more than twelve million immigrants, with more on the way. What will become of the Argentine Republic when, as now seems probable, the number of new arrivals surpasses the number of native-born citizens? The Congress and all our public authorities can then congratulate themselves on having avoided the slightest embarrassment to the new arrivals!

It is notable that such embarrassment did not prevent twelve million immigrants—including English, French, and Germans—from gaining citizenship in the United States, and without making the slightest objection concerning imagined injuries to their dignity. How different is our situation, in which a few hundred thousand foreign nationals seek to impose a law on our Congress, as if they were negotiating a treaty between sovereign nations. What a generous offer they make to us! We will rule you as long as we don't have to request the privilege of doing so!

Really?

The current initiative's lack of careful logic is distressing. For example, its proponents speak of "foreigners," an excessively general category for our purposes. Some "foreigners" are completely temporary residents, though possibly long term, such as the managers of English or French commercial houses. Properly speaking, such a person is not an emigrant, nor is he an immigrant. Also a "foreigner" is the man who truly emigrated from his country of origin years ago to settle, put down roots as they say, in the Argentine Republic. Finally, a third sort of "foreigner," whose presence here may or may not be transient because it depends on the unstable economic forces in play, includes short-term contract workers, the poor, raw, and unskilled working-class arrivals of recent years, something like two hundred thousand of them in the last five years.

Monsieur Peusser, one of the sponsors of the initiative, is a "foreigner" of the second category. But what is appropriate for him would not be appropriate for other "foreigners," although no distinction is made by proponents of the measure.

In addition, adoption of the proposed measure would create an anomalous group within our body politic: individuals who can enjoy the immunities of a foreign national in Argentina, such as exemption from military service, but who might, at any moment, activate their automatic status as Argentine citizens, without ever having requested that status or declared their intention to embrace it. These "automatic citizens" would enjoy an advantage that the merely native-born would lack—the ability to go incognito, so to speak.

Granting automatic citizenship to those who have truly emigrated from their countries of origin is, then, much less objectionable than granting it to an undifferentiated mass of "foreigners." The problem is distinguishing the individuals who may be properly termed "immigrants." In practical terms, how is the distinction administered? A number of years of residence is normally part of the formula, two being traditional in American republics. What document must the automatic citizen present at the polls? Is it possible for automatically activated citizenship to be deactivated when the recipient no longer wishes to exercise the corresponding responsibilities and privileges? And if so, can that deactivation be automatic, without requesting it, and if so, I ask—how will it be known that the deactivation has occurred?

This initiative has no redeeming characteristics. It amounts to giving away the country.

The Dignity of Foreigners: Some Final Thoughts

I have in fact heard some men of consequence say, in all sincerity, that they feel it somewhat indecorous to request or make application for Argentine citizenship because it suggests a kind of disloyalty, a faithless abandonment of the nationality of the birth. This opinion arises from a mistaken analysis of the issues, and the hundreds of foreigners who support the arguments made by this newspaper clamor for clarification, certain that their countrymen of goodwill will agree with them once the matter has been adequately explained.

At present, foreigners can already acquire Argentine citizenship after two years' residence by merely requesting it. Therefore, those who believe that the proposed measure gives them access to citizenship are mistaken. It can only "give them access" if they currently lack it. Furthermore, existing regulations require that on specific occasions, a letter of citizenship must be presented to the authorities. In fact, our constitution would have to be amended in order to make citizenship "automatic." Article 20 says explicitly that foreign nationals in Argentina who wish to acquire citizenship can nonetheless remain exempt from compulsory military service for ten years from the time of issuance of their letter of citizenship! So, no letter, no exemption! Perhaps the campaign in favor of automatic citizenship should warn its supposed beneficiaries that they might as well prepare to be drafted!

Another hazard so far insufficiently discussed, in view of the absence of agreed-upon documentation to constrain the mercurial possibilities of automatic citizenship, is massive voter fraud, which can logically only be encouraged thereby.

Lastly, let us consider how likely it is that people who daily need to interact with the civil authorities on the basis of legal documentation will be embarrassed to have it on hand. Will the two hundred thousand current candidates (and the four million on the way) who are illiterate and have only dim notions of constitutional government really find it beneath their dignity to request constitutional exercise of the greatest right of all, which is the right of self-government? How can that be offensive to one's dignity, properly understood?

To live in someone else's house, to be governed not by one's self, but by others—*that* is an offense to one's dignity, properly understood. To remain aloof from the struggle to destroy Indian predators and open the southern and western frontiers for peaceful, productive settlement—that is offensive, as well. To accept automatically into our political community a large uncontrolled population that hopes to maintain its overseas ties indefinitely in a kind of dual citizenship that will exist or not at the unspoken whim of its possessor—that is offensive to our national dignity, and dangerous to our national future.

Obras, vo. 36, pp. 192–97

5. Civilization in Daily Life

Sarmiento famously defined civilization partly in contradistinction to rural, native culture. On the other hand, his brief commentaries and essays on newspapers, theater, daily play, carnival, and the construction of rail lines provide alternative, prescriptive definitions of civilization and civilized behavior. Many of his attitudes are predictable, but some are surprising. For example, Sarmiento *liked* the carnival water fight others considered barbarous. The most important example of civilization in daily life was public education. While being the caudillo of the press was Sarmiento's main claim to fame, his role as the primary architect of public primary education in Argentina was another one, and far from minor. By 1900, Argentina (and Uruguay) had become home to the most successful public education systems in Latin America. Sarmiento was at the very center of this initiative, for it was critical to his vision of a civilized nation, as we see in his comments dealing with the creation of normal schools and the connections between home, the *patria*, and female students. Ultimately, a civilized Argentina was only possible through public education. Women teachers and students were imperative to the success of this aspiration.

5. Civilization in Daily Life
"On Reading Newspapers,"
in *El Mercurio*, 4 July and 7 August 1841[1]

The question is really not why our publications are few. There is a good explanation. Let us examine that question a bit more, however, before answering and going beyond it.

The question is irksome when one contemplates the expansion of periodical publications in the nineteenth century, tracing the intimate connections between liberty, civilization, material progress, and intellectual growth. The question becomes more urgent when one observes how the press undermines thrones and topples despots, how it serves in republics as the chief bulwark of civil liberties, an important check on the behavior of administrators. The question nags at us during any public consideration of conflictive issues requiring wide dissemination of basic information, requiring too that diverse opinions be aired. The question becomes acute when one looks at the overall situation of Chile, which is particularly backward in this crucial arena of national progress.

Countries such as ours have a particular need for a vigorous and active periodical press. Our people are uneducated and would benefit by the information that newspapers can provide. Our people lack an awareness of their common participation in a national community, as well as a sufficient understanding of the basic principles of republican governance. Newspapers are the key to that awareness and understanding, just as they facilitate commerce, stimulate industry, and awaken the entrepreneurial spirit. The periodical press recognizes achievement, condemns wrongdoing, coordinates myriad social activities, and informs the public regarding norms and decrees. But the existence of many newspapers by itself will not achieve these praiseworthy purposes, without the existence of a wide readership.

The lack of such a readership is, I believe, the root of the problem in countries like ours. We have few newspapers, and their content is minimal, because they lack readers. Whatever the origin of this situation, the relative absence of a reading public must be accounted an embarrassment for a nation that has begun to distinguish itself, among its sister

---

1. In this 1841 Valparaíso newspaper column written during his exile in Chile, Sarmiento laments that most press activity in the country (which he provisionally adopts, here, as "our country") is linked to elections, so that periodical publications' enormous potential for public betterment remains unrealized. With the conclusion of elections, *El Mercurio* (for which he writes) will apparently again be the only newspaper in Chile.

5. Civilization in Daily Life

republics of South America, for its exemplary public order and stability. Governments that obey the rule of a despot will naturally discourage the circulation of many newspapers, but such is not Chile's case. Why does a country characterized by peace, prosperity, a thriving overseas trade, and an enviable degree of institutional consolidation, a country that extends its influence over its neighbors day by day—why, I repeat, does a country such as this, well into the nineteenth century, have only one daily newspaper of limited circulation?

Can you imagine what opinion a modern European visitor must form of us? A modern European for whom the periodical press constitutes an index of cultural achievement, a touchstone of civilization. Or perhaps a visitor from the United States of America, for whom a vigorous periodical press is synonymous with liberty and prosperity? Such a visitor to our shores will see virtually nothing to remind them of the burgeoning one thousand five hundred newspapers and magazines published today in the United States, arriving eventually at the remotest farmhouse. Visitors who equate newspapers with progress may form too harsh a judgment of us, admittedly. Yet who can blame them, given the basic outlines of the matter.

One example, albeit extreme, can stand for many: Boston. Useful statistics indicate that in the year 1834, Boston (not including the entire state of Massachusetts, which has other cities of consideration) had forty-three newspapers and twenty-two monthly magazines, six annual almanacs, and a wide variety of other periodical publications appearing annually, semiannually, bimonthly, or weekly, for a total of no fewer than ninety periodical publications that found a sufficient number of subscribers in a city of eighty thousand inhabitants. Other cities of the United States can boast similarly prodigious statistics, and even smaller towns have a vigorous periodical press, putting a limit on the circulation of any individual publication.

Consider the following comparison between Boston and the Republic of Chile. Boston is a single city with eighty thousand inhabitants, as we have had occasion to mention already. The Republic of Chile is a sprawling territorial entity that comprises over a million inhabitants. Boston is one city in one state of the North American federation—and not the capital of that state. Chile is a sovereign nation, among the most successful in South America today. And here's Boston, with forty-three newspapers! And Chile with one.

And what about our youth, you may well ask, whose responsibility it is to set an example, thereby improving our national culture so that Chile

5. Civilization in Daily Life

may take a rightful place among the civilized nations of the earth? Are they devoted readers of the periodicals that sum up, for better or for worse, the basic facts of our day and age? Unfortunately, our intellectual youth demonstrates its refined judgment by considering Chilean periodicals beneath them. One cannot quarrel with the critic who finds them mediocre. But a higher level of journalism would be unlikely to attract a larger readership. The greater refinement desired by our golden youth would probably restrict the readership even more. The modern nineteenth-century press directs itself to a mass audience; its overall cultural level—language, allusions, taste—cannot exceed that of its mass audience.

One can always find food to feed a healthy curiosity in the periodical press. I don't dispute the criticisms of our modest editorial production. The news itself is the most important information in the newspaper. The events of our age never cease to amaze the discerning observer, and their general direction shows a clear affinity from one country to the next in this ever-more-interconnected world. What happens in distant lands now threatens to affect our own well-being. The threat of war in Europe will certainly impact the march of civilization in the world as a whole. Egypt, the ancient land at the center of the conflict, is shaking off the dust of forgetfulness to resume its honored place in the march of civilization. In Spain, the forces of liberal reform and clerical reaction grapple in mortal combat. Closer at hand, our sister republics of Spanish America present a lamentable picture, from Mexico to Argentina. Familiar ideas and interests clash in these republics, and their social process is similar to our own. Their failures and successes, villains and heroes, are ultimately ours as well. We cannot but be spectators to their news! And yet still, where are the readers?

Ah, but let a partisan political contest roil our national waters, and newspapers appear out of nowhere, opening offices on every street, furiously praising this or that candidate. Such ephemeral publications, with their lack of serious journalism, debase our public life. Each and every partisan rag loudly announces its patriotic mission without ever contributing to any project of civic improvement. Where is the discussion of modern social theories? Where are the practical proposals for bettering the popular classes, improving public education or sanitation or morality? Where is the awareness that Chile has undergone a political revolution with social implications? Is it any wonder that the condition of the popular classes leaves so much to be desired in both material and spiritual terms? Is it any wonder that the expansion of economic activity has been so slow?

5. Civilization in Daily Life

Let us not blame the government for this state of affairs. Transformations of the sort that Chile requires cannot occur without the active support of an informed citizenry. If the state of our periodical press is not appropriate to the necessities of a great nation, the fault lies only within ourselves. Chile's newspapers could easily expand in coverage, multiply in number, and improve in quality, if only the tiny size of their readership did not make irrelevant—and ultimately, doom—any attempted reform.

Obras, vol. 1, pp. 75–79

"On Theater and Cultural Criticism," in *El Mercurio*, 8 November 1841

One crucial function of periodical publications, a function that, if more seriously undertaken, could truly energize our national press, is cultural criticism. I refer not only to commentary on the quality of theatrical performances that traveling companies bring to our shores from time to time, but to a much broader function. A cultural critic discusses social customs and social vices, corrects common but erroneous ways of speaking that come to characterize a particular population, and promotes new ideas, addressing popular misconceptions that must be cleared away to facilitate progressive social change.

Today Chile enjoys peace in the wake of our wars of independence. The country is now endowed with the necessary framework of governmental institutions. The system has begun to function. What is the next necessary step in the successful establishment of our republic?

The next step is to see how our republic works in practice and, through observation, analysis, and incremental improvement, perfect our institutions and our liberty, facilitating our further progress and economic development. The press can and must contribute to the process by engaging in intelligent, constructive criticism. The press can and must be the chief agent by which our society raises its general level of civilization. More precisely, the press can and must identify the social actors and social behaviors that stand in the way of progress, discrediting them in the eyes of its readership.

Cultural criticism is such an important activity that one desires to see our most gifted young writers engage in it. They must not be too easily discouraged by the uneven results of their initial attempts, however, nor by the difficulty of the task that lies ahead. A willingness to criticize, sometimes boldly, is required by the situation. Only bold criticism, as long as it is well founded, will awaken Chile from its current lethargy and move it toward its democratic destiny. They make a great mistake, writers who decline to publish bold criticisms for fear that they lack the necessary intelligence or learning, degree or rank. Of course the critics, too, will be criticized. Those who do this important work must not allow themselves to be cowed by fear of criticism from the established arbiters of taste and conventional wisdom.

Our republic is in its infancy, and so too is our national press. The roughness and imperfections of our public discourse are a true reflection of our national condition. Only rough and imperfect publications can be popular and democratic in today's Chile. Let the societies of Europe direct their energies to cultivating niceties of poetry and prose. To do so in Chile shows an author to be more self-absorbed than patriotic. We in Chile must perfect the functioning of our republic, not the purity of literary forms that our people are still far from appreciating.

Obras, vol. 1, pp. 147–48

"Christmas Eve Celebrations,"
in *El Mercurio*, 26 December 1841

Last night I struggled to get to sleep for about an hour, mindful of the rest required to put in a good day's work, but it was hopeless. The city's night watchmen declared themselves unable to quiet the raucous cries of large groups of people who augmented their voices with horns, whistles, drums, and various sorts of noisemakers. In other words, Santiago's traditional Christmas Eve celebrations promised their usual delights, and, having lost all hope of sleeping, I resolved to be part of the festivities. So I abandoned my comfortable, celibate bedchamber and, following a five-minute engagement with mirror and washstand, emerged into the street.

A remarkable spectacle awaited me there. Despite the advanced hour, the streets were thronged with people in straw hats walking around aimlessly. The disorder of their movements, the shrillness of their cries, the

5. Civilization in Daily Life

evident inability of dozens of church bells, sounding all at once, to make themselves heard above the general din—everything, in other words, seemed more indicative of a disaster or emergency than a joyous religious commemoration.

The large public clock that, in recent years, has served the inhabitants of our fair city to regulate and coordinate their collective activities managed to make itself heard by striking twelve midnight, whereupon the general din grew even louder. The crowd grew denser as it flowed in the direction of the cathedral and midnight mass. The jostling crush provided opportunity and cover for fervent declarations of love by young men who had worked all evening to get their arms around the object of their affections. Women exercising the function of chaperone strained to hear what was said in hopes of policing the purity of their young charges as we pressed through the door into the church without pews.

Mass was just beginning. Well-dressed young men moved incessantly through the crowd without devoting the slightest bit of attention to the mass itself. Instead, they directed their entire interest to certain well-dressed young women, to whom, stopping occasionally in their perambulations, the young men directed an obscure performance repeated with minor variations at each stop. The young women could rarely enjoy the performance unmolested, however, because their mothers' sharp elbows kept the daughter's eyes focused instead on the mystery of the Eucharist.

Barely had I made the previous observation when the mass ended and the crowd flowed out into the street again. As we passed a basin of holy water, I wet my finger and crossed myself against uncharitable thoughts. But I could not pause long in the church door without getting shoved and trampled by the faithful. As I emerged into the wee hours of Christmas morning, a new spectacle challenged the composure of my faith. I found the cold, hard steps of the atrium crowded with people, poor Chileans whom I can only presume to be Catholics, sleeping. They were not allowed to enter the temple, I was told, because of their clothes. How horrid!

The cool breeze and large, high moon calmed me down and, as a couple of hours remained before dawn, I decided to give my skinny legs some exercise after standing so long during mass. On an impulse I turned around and set a course for one of our city's great civilized adornments, the Alameda Boulevard.

On the Alameda, chaos reigned, and the popular classes were its obedient subjects. Fights and drunken arguments could be heard everywhere, rocks flew back and forth through the air, men had begun the game of

5. Civilization in Daily Life

snatching away women's shawls—while such police as existed were too few to have any discernible impact on the crowd. I had taken only a few steps along the promenade when a ragged fellow carrying a tray of food for sale approached too close for comfort. "And what'll it be? Milk punch? Horchata? Fermented aloja, nice and fizzy? No? How about fried fish? Beet salad? What'll it be?"

I told him to let me be, and the ignorant fool took offense. "So we have a fancy-pants gentleman, do we?" And I was obliged to teach the wretch a lesson, though I had cause to regret the attempt. The ragged fellow dropped his tray and jerked my hat down over my eyes almost to my mouth, requiring five minutes for me to extricate my head and quite ruining the hat.

No use in even thinking to call for a night watchman, of course. Who could have heard my cries above the merry din? Meanwhile the ragged fellow had not gone away and was rolling up his sleeves, loudly preparing to pound me to a pulp. Prudence, more than fear, dictated my departure from the Alameda. I found myself in a small, quiet plaza patrolled by a night watchman who seemed in control of the situation. Saved! In the predawn darkness, I contemplated the ruins of the old royal mint for a few minutes before heading in the direction of the river bridge, where I hoped to find the pedestrians better behaved than those of the Alameda. Instead I came upon a vehicle carrying bodies to the morgue. This was too much! My hair stood on end as I contemplated the misery of these men's families. Christmas Eve celebrations, indeed!

Now I began to see more ragged people herding their dirty pack animals through the still dark streets, roughly joking, singing snatches of ribald ballads, bringing meat and produce to market. They were not few nor did they move slowly, carrying provisions for eighty thousand inhabitants of Santiago. It was an amazing sight, an entire world previously unglimpsed by me. Who could understand all their terms of art? They had everything, it seemed, all big, beautiful, and fresh.

Across the plaza, another group of people was arriving—those who had celebrated Christmas Eve all night. They did not, in truth, look their best. The mission of each scruffy gallant was to purchase a carnation for his scruffy damsel, presumably in payment or at least recompense for services already rendered. It was a sellers' market, and stalls with flowers for sale took full advantage of the buyers' inability to bargain. A number of market stalls had put out small tables and endowed them with filthy tablecloths where elegant breakfasters could imbibe something that made them sputter loudly after each gulp.

How many pretty faces did I see that morning, faces that had once made my heart beat excitedly, that I never again found attractive! Decent young ladies of Santiago, do not go out to celebrate Christmas Eve all night if you value your reputation! Your delicate faces will lose their innocence in the ribald revelry. I would say more, but I fear to offend your mothers, who have no more business in the street at that hour than do their daughters.

And you, elegant young men of the nineteenth century, why do you attend these so-called Christmas Eve celebrations? To disrupt the mass? And why do you go after midnight to the Alameda? To participate in vile acts of drunkenness and prostitution? To mix with the sort of people who would be in jail if our constabulary had the wit and energy to jail them?

Decent young people of Santiago, leave the lower classes to their disgraceful entertainments, at least until the police find the wherewithal to eliminate the worst abuses and disorder. As for me, I promise that you'll not see me in that questionable crowd ever again, or at least, until I get a new hat.

Obras, vol. 1, pp. 158–61

"The Theater, a Tool of Cultural Education," in *El Mercurio*, 20 June 1842

This is not the first time that we address readers about a matter that our government has always ignored totally, a crucial element of our social organization: the theater. The government has failed to recognize the importance of promoting the theater, abandoning it, instead, to whatever development may occur randomly and spontaneously. This is a grave error.

The theater is not simply a public entertainment or spectacle, comparable to a cockfight or the circus. The theater performs a far more important, and one can safely say higher, social function than does a cockfight or the circus because, more than a simple diversion, it is a way to educate both heart and mind. The theater is admittedly not an outlet for our own dramaturgy, as things stand today, because touring companies from abroad present the great majority of theatrical productions. Fomenting local theatrical efforts would be worthwhile, but it should

5. Civilization in Daily Life

constitute a long-term objective. In the meantime, the theater still fulfills the crucial function of providing us with our best window on the world beyond our shores.

In particular, traveling European companies acquaint Chilean theatergoers with the salient works and themes of the two theatrical traditions most relevant to the needs of our own society: the Spanish theater and the French theater. What better way to become acquainted with complex modern trends than to "listen in," so to speak, on the introductions that the playwrights of Spain and France have provided for their own people. And not only do modern works speak to the current state of affairs. In addition, modern theater takes its social responsibilities seriously, producing works that are actively didactic and aimed at cultural improvement. Even here, far from the center of Western theatrical culture, people sense that playwrights have assumed a special role as social critics and teachers. The old tragedies and comedies of manners are out of sync with the age and have been replaced by plays with a different sensibility, of which the most familiar to us, because of their centrality to the contemporary Spanish theatrical repertory, are the works of Bretón de los Herreros.

All of his works promote a progressive principle or criticize some sort of retrograde resistance to progress. And the same principles and the same sorts of resistance obtain equally in Spain and in Chile. The modern nineteenth-century theater of Spain and France attacks tyranny of all kinds, whether in the public square or in domestic life. It supports individual liberty for both men and women. It supports meritocracy and decries emphasis on social class and class hierarchy. For these reasons, and because the dramatic traditions of France and Spain have so many traditional points of contact, French and Spanish theater offers an unsurpassed opportunity to treat the origins of contemporary social ills and raise the cultural level of the Chilean population as a whole. While many other observations may be made about the French and Spanish plays presented in Santiago by traveling companies, nothing else is nearly so important.

Where is there another activity of equal social significance? Where, more than in the theater, do citizens of all social classes, occupying diverse places in our social hierarchy, gather with a single purpose, sharing the same notions, the same sensations, the same pleasures? Is the government not gratified to see international performers bring us samples of the cultural transformations now occurring in the world's most advanced societies? Is it not gratified to see actors tread local stages to speak lines penned in Europe by Victor Hugo, Alexandre Dumas, Mariano José de

5. Civilization in Daily Life

Larra, and Manuel Bretón de los Herreros? Is the government not gratified to see famous international works presented by international actors who have come to Chile because they believe that we will appreciate their art? Does it mistake the value of musical performances, especially opera? No? In that case, our governmental authorities at every level from the municipality on up ought to explain *what they have done* to help the theater achieve its lofty mission in Chile. Let the municipalities of Santiago and Valparaíso respond, above all.

What? No response?

That is precisely correct. They have done nothing, nothing at all! Neither Santiago nor Valparaíso even possesses a structure appropriate for theatrical presentations. Valparaíso uses a *corral,* as they call it, which may be large enough, but has none of the special characteristics needed for a proper theatrical production, and the same may be said of the large *patio* where plays are performed in the capital of Chile, a venue so precarious that its owners may destine it for another purpose at any moment. It would appear that the theater was very recently arrived in Chile, because it has yet to find even a permanent home, and one would not be surprised to see it pull up stakes, tomorrow, to go somewhere that will better appreciate it.

Meanwhile, the police vainly try to control the self-destructive elements of proletarian life, such as drunkenness and a taste for gambling that destroy in a few hours the much-needed wages of a week's hard work. And yet, these wretches, too, need and deserve diversion.

An enlightened government facilitates productive, beneficial sorts of diversion for the popular classes. It provides appropriate venues for popular diversions, and above all, it builds theaters and promotes theatrical activities of all kinds, because they constitute so much more than a simple diversion. The theater improves, enlightens, educates. Its doors are open to men who seek to improve themselves, men of all walks of life, men whose achievements may be commercial or military or intellectual. Frustrate their ambitions, provide no form of social advancement for such men, and you will have problems. He who might have been inspired to patriotic glory becomes a bandit. He who might have become an industrialist, creating wealth, prefers gambling and speculations, turning his ingenuity to crime.

What are they thinking, the governments that decline to build theaters large enough to admit all comers for a reasonable price? Do they realize that, in so doing, they drive thousands of young men into destructive activities that lead nowhere positive? Don't they realize that the grandeur

5. Civilization in Daily Life

and nobility of the structure itself communicates the value and dignity of what happens therein? Don't they understand that the presence of a diverse public, the enchantment of the presentation itself, and the challenge of new ideas would combine to create a superior citizenry for our republic? Have they calculated the cost—in inveterate ignorance and backwardness—of their inaction?

Alas, no.

Obras, vol. 1, pp. 271–75

"Goodbye to Carnival!"
in *El Mercurio*, 10 February 1842

The final three days before Lent used to be, above all, the three days of carnival. No longer. The practices associated with our traditional carnival celebrations—with their secure place on the Catholic calendar, despite their pagan inspiration and the disfavor of popes—have been prohibited by the authorities of Santiago. We are left with simply the "final three days" before Lent. The gaping hole left by the disappearance of our traditional festival has not been filled, in our capital city, by masked balls or other admittedly more modern and elegant carnival activities typical of Rome and, above all, Venice. What has been gained by this no doubt well-intentioned reform?

There is no good answer, only a flood of questions to go with the flood of water that used to fly through the air during the three final days. Does anyone not remember the childlike joy with which both men and women put aside straitlaced conventionalism for three days each year? What old boy has forgotten the thrill of seeing a girl's shapely contours, so impossible to trace on all the other days of the year, by wetting her clothes during a carnival water fight? Who among my gentlemanly readers does not recall the satisfaction to be had—years ago, of course—by dumping a full bucket of not-always-crystal-clear water over the head of the sputtering, gesticulating chaperone assigned, all the other days of the year, to keep young bucks like him at a safe distance from the objects of their desire? What buck, young or old, needing to say a few words into the ear of his beloved, doesn't regret the disappearance of the carnival water fight that offered so many opportunities to get close? First, separate her from the

5. Civilization in Daily Life

herd, chase her through that door. Perfect. Now she's cornered, begging for mercy, but she never showed any mercy. Speak if you must, but it is preferable to act. Wet her good! A negotiated surrender ought to involve a kiss. Who, I ask you, does not get agitated and weak-kneed remembering the great battles of the sexes, when water flew in all directions through an atmosphere thick with girls' shrieks and boys' guffaws, until the losers slipped and tumbled, possibly tangled together with the winners, into muddy puddles that dimmed the glory of the most radiant goddess?

Those were the good old days! You could never offer a young lady your arm, back then, nor dare to speak aloud certain compliments that today raise no eyebrows, but during three days of the year, the oppressive limitations of Spanish tradition were held in abeyance. During the carnival melee one could speak to the girls, possibly melt an icy heart through demonstration of ardor and eloquence, and, best of all, touch them without fear and apply the irresistible advantage of superior masculine muscles. Among gallants, these were days of brotherhood and equality. To visit a young woman's house a suitor required no invitation and introduction, as long as he was ready to endure the inevitable dousing with undaunted good humor.

Now everything is more dignified and less fun. The final three days before Lent have lost the jovial frankness, the innocent lack of inhibition, that once characterized them. Here in Santiago it is still permitted, and even encouraged, for men to flirt aggressively with women in the street and perhaps sprinkle them with a few drops of perfume in the process. Only in the provincial towns of Chile do the unbridled older customs retain any of their old vigor. No further outside the capital than Peñaflor, for example, you'll notice (in addition to purer air) that some of the old liberty (the traditional approximation between sexes and social classes) still operates.

Carnival in Peñaflor is a permanent state of excitement. Guitars everywhere thrum with the distinctive rhythm of our national dance music, bringing a smile to everyone's lips and a mysterious mobility to everyone's hips. Amorous secrets swell in every heart. If you go to Peñaflor for carnival, be sure to greet all the girls with the attention that they merit (all of them), casting aside social prejudices. Yes, I know, you've never met these girls. I realize that you've not been properly introduced. No matter. You will be the best of friends, at least until carnival ends, laughing and dancing. Then you'll ride back to Santiago, singing the ribald lyrics that they taught you, deciding what you'll say about carnival in Peñaflor, whether it was fabulous or lame. And either way, don't expect the beauties of

5. Civilization in Daily Life

Peñaflor to recognize you or say hello when you meet them later on the streets of Santiago, because what happens in Peñaflor, stays in Peñaflor.

As for the final three days in Santiago, what do we have left? They signal the end of school holidays, when students must return to the unwelcome task of memorizing information of no use in the present and only uncertain application to the future. And they signal a time for the entire swarm of lawyers and judges and clerks and litigants to put away their pens and parchments for a while and give their delicate consciences a rest. And that's all. However well-intentioned, the reforms have left us nothing to replace the delights of the old days. The reformers found old dances like the chaconne a bit too risqué for modern tastes, but the diversions that they put in its place, formal masked balls in which each man adopts a costume representing a well-known figure from fiction, history, or the theater, or whatever—just isn't carnival. And because few women are willing to wear costumes, the masked balls become a pointless guessing game that separates the sexes rather than bringing them together. The result is insipid and dreary.

Here is one point on which the inhabitants of Buenos Aires have the advantage over those of Santiago. Well-intentioned social innovations have been few under the steady hand of the illustrious Restorer of the Laws, who has taken care to cater to popular tastes that are often quite traditional. And popular tastes are unequivocal in the matter. According to vox populi in both Argentina and Chile, carnival is a sacred right, basic to human life, an imperious social necessity. Therefore, Rosas has so far not interfered with traditional carnival practices in Buenos Aires. Therefore, believe it or not, the Rosas administration has taken a number of laudable measures to regulate what it has not cared to prohibit.

At nine o'clock in the morning on each of the three days of carnival, a cannon fires to signal the beginning of the water fight, and a thousand shouts can be heard on all sides, and the common people of Buenos Aires throng the streets, heedlessly and promiscuously mixed, en masse. Young and old, male and female, black and white, clerks and stevedores are carrying the munitions specific to this kind of warfare. Water with perfume, water from ditches, water-squirting syringes the size of a man's arm, and especially baskets of water-bearing projectiles fashioned from eggs. The yoke and white have been removed through a small hole, replaced with water, and the hole plugged with a drop of wax. When launching such a projectile, the experienced carnival reveler rarely misses his mark. Males aim chiefly at females, and vice versa, but there are other popular targets, as well. God help anyone, of whatever rank or dignity, even an

5. Civilization in Daily Life

ambassador or a high court judge, who tries to make his way through these streets elegantly attired in recent European styles. Those who pose, in Buenos Aires, as "the sovereign people," constantly incited by a band of inveterate pro-Rosas cutthroats, do not take kindly to "fancy-pants" gentlemen who "think they are better" than the common people. An in-your-face tailcoat will immediately attract the ire of these egalitarian arbiters of taste and, along with their ire, a veritable deluge of projectiles, covering the expensive garment with various slimy and repulsive liquids, to which a million tiny fragments of eggshell adhere semipermanently. Should this happen to you, be very careful not to betray the slightest hint of disapproval, otherwise you'll be declared a "filthy and disgusting" enemy of the regime, with no limit to what the vulgar throng might do next.

Once the citywide battle has been fully joined, every house becomes a castle, its rooftop terrace and its balconies become parapets, and the street below seethes with besiegers. The girls who patrol the battlements rain pails of water on the besiegers, the most daring of whom bring in siege ladders. Every aspect of human ingenuity is brought to bear, including various sorts of water traps for the unsuspecting. One tried-and-true technique is to post a large sign with showy lettering on some strategic street corner and wait until a cluster of curious readers gathers before launching the deluge on their heads. And if you see an object, possibly a money bag, lying on the pavement—don't stoop to pick it up, please! There are also siege engines capable of dousing the lovely defenders on the battlements. In other words, an English visitor to Buenos Aires carnival today will find indisputable progress when comparing the phenomena just described with an earlier English account of 1806. Back then, according to no less an authority than Sir Walter Scott, we in Buenos Aires all lived in dirt-floor huts furnished only with cow skulls to sit on and rawhide flaps to cover the door.

The general din is infernal. Adding to it, you can expect drummers who detect your sensitivity to follow you all over town beating and beating their drums. The more it plainly annoys you, the louder they beat and beat and beat their drums, and the more you try to escape, the more closely they will follow. Glowering at them and waving your arms are useless. The only remedy is to put your hand in your pocket and pay them well for all the trouble they have taken with you. Still, there is a smile on every face, for this is the great mass of the common people at carefree play, enjoying a holiday from their daily labors, feeling confident about their claim to public space, enjoying a sense of equality with anyone

5. Civilization in Daily Life

else in the street. This eminently plebeian crowd—poetic, ebullient, and bellicose—abandons itself totally to this make-believe civil war. Well might they prefer this bloodless simulacrum to the real wars they've endured for a generation.

Finally, the cannon's shot echoes through the city, interrupting the game until tomorrow. Attackers and defenders immediately stop. The hands that brandished a water-filled egg in the street, ready to hurl it with deadly accuracy, pocket the munition for tomorrow. The hands that had assembled brimful pails and pans on the balcony leave them in place until tomorrow. The ceasefire is remarkably complete. Girls unwilling to risk their elegant dresses on the street before now, suddenly appear at windows and in doorways. And woe be to him who allows the merest drop of water to fly from his hand now. Police respond with alacrity to discipline anyone accused of violating the ceasefire.

What do we have in Santiago to compare with carnival in Buenos Aires? Let me say only that, when we get around to canceling well-intentioned reforms that create no improvement over certain tried-and-true traditions, I suggest that traditional carnival games be the first thing that we restore. After that, how about the religious processions with penitents and dancing devils!

Obras, vol. 1, pp. 339–44

"Carnival of 1857,"
in *El Nacional*, 25 February 1857

The press is pleased to call attention to a positive development in this year's carnival activities.

Carnival matters, because the common people of Buenos Aires have few occasions for collective celebration, and this one is good for them. Rosista repression masqueraded as excessive tranquility. An occasional expression of rowdy high spirits is not symptomatic of a social ill. Our first president, Rivadavia, prohibited traditional carnival activities such as the water game to reshape our republic following the lead of progressive European countries. The Rosista reaction against Rivadavian Europhilia brought back the water game and even further institutionalized it. They say that Rosas himself took part in the street reveling, dressed in a Pampa

5. Civilization in Daily Life

Indian poncho. But the anarchic freedom of the carnival spirit always risks going too far. Some sort of mockery suffered by the great man, or one of his minions, turned the regime implacably against the carnival celebrations, which were banned as a result. The fall of Rosas brought carnival roaring back, however, and the celebrations have now been evolving.

And that is really the news here. What we might call "the aquatic dimension" of the celebrations has declined notably in importance. The first two days of street reveling passed without cause for lamentation. Indeed, an ever-increasing part of street play involves throwing flowers or confections in paper wrappers. Evidently, the cost of these improved munitions also improves the class of people who can afford to take part in the street reveling. In addition, carriages with well-dressed occupants have become much more numerous than costumed men on horseback. So far, we have had no news of the kind of regrettable accident, the fruit of various kinds of excess, that have marred carnival games in years past.

Carnival must be civilized because it cannot be abolished. It provides an opportunity to blow off steam, a necessity of the human spirit which has to be satisfied in one way or another. If Sunday were not a day of rest, we'd need another one. Likewise, if people were not allowed to thumb their noses at propriety during carnival, they would find another, very possibly more destructive, way to undermine propriety. Carnival is useful, as well, because it provides an authentic collective self-portrait. Far more than an election, so full of posturing, carnival shows us to ourselves as we really are. That is why the positive evolution of activities this year merits, or even demands, our applause.

Buenos Aires carnival this year began to resemble what goes on during those same three days in advanced European countries. No fewer than five or six different theaters have organized masked balls, and there has not been a single problem worth mentioning in any of them. Even the stately Colón Theater opened the doors to its spacious salons, allowing the public to delight in marvelous decorations of the latest Parisian fashion, illuminated by a thousand gas jets that, together, approximated the light of the sun. True, on the first night the better class of patrons held itself aloof from the bulk of unknown (and masked) revelers, but on the third night their reluctance seemed vanish, and the crowd of three thousand, including members of the most distinguished families of Buenos Aires society, mixed together happily.

It is a significant thing to gather the people of Buenos Aires, rich and poor, who have so frequently fought against one another, and see them associating so easily and intimately on the dance floor. In the carnival crowd of the last night there were no social distinctions, no separation, and no policing except for each individual's attention to good manners and decorum. This, ladies and gentlemen, is an advance in civilization. Gathered in the palatial salons of the Colón Theater, surrounded by gold leaf, the sovereign people feel the nobility, the sovereignty that ought to be theirs in a republic such as ours. Their surroundings raise their spirits to the level inspired by the art and architecture. In contrast, before the French Revolution, the king of that country marked certain holidays by throwing handfuls of candy to crowds of commoners who dove to the ground and squabbled over whatever it was, like a pack of hounds.

Common people who are treated like dogs will learn to regard themselves that way. Our democracy, on the other hand, aims to raise people up, to offer them the finer things that were once available only to the aristocracy. Half a century ago, the lavish architecture of the Colón Theater would have been considered appropriate for European princes. Today, we consider it appropriate for the citizenry of Buenos Aires. And circumstances endorse our judgment. The exhibition of its salons was an economic success for the Colón Theater. Its enormous expenditures on mirrors and bronzes and gold leaf accurately anticipated a new age, when the populace of Buenos Aires would begin to acquire a civic culture appropriate to a world-class city. Our budding metropolis is about to come of age. The sound of locomotives perturbs the atmosphere and celebrated European performers add us to their international itineraries. The word is out. There now exists in Buenos Aires a cultivated public capable of appreciating the arts and developing the country's resources.

The carnival celebration of 1857 has inaugurated a new level of progress in our civic culture. In a word, the common people have shown themselves to be worthy of republican liberty. Even troublesome partisan tensions that could be felt on the eve of carnival seemed to dissipate during the revelry. Notably, the leaders of various contending factions moved freely among the crowds of masked revelers in the streets, and though, to my knowledge, all had their faces uncovered, no masked adversary violated the carnival spirit of play to launch a serious attack. In other words, this year's carnival has shown us a rather surprising, and infinitely desirable, improvement in ourselves. Congratulations, Buenos Aires!

Obras, vol. 24, pp. 213–16

5. Civilization in Daily Life

"The Railroad Linking Buenos Aires to San Fernando: A Public Address Delivered 17 August 1859"

Fellow Citizens:

We have just broken ground on a construction project of vast significance. Today we began the creation of the first link of an iron chain that will eventually extend the civilizing action of commerce to a significant portion of our national territory, binding together the diverse areas of settlement along the Plata, Pilcomayo, and Bermejo Rivers. It is high time that we did so.

The Spanish Crown, upon taking possession of our America, concerned itself very little about the fate of towns that it had founded, during a century of exploration and conquest, in the vast peripheral expanses of its New World empire. The Spanish conquerors were dauntless, but motivated by visions of personal gain and glory, always seeking further conquests. Pizarro's followers had hardly brought down the Inca empire when they set off to conquer Chile. Hardly had they established their first outpost on Santa Lucia peak, founding what is today Santiago, than they sent a party of sixty lancers to cross the Andes and found Mendoza and San Juan on the other side. Solís, the leader of the first Spanish expedition to enter the Río de la Plata, paused only briefly in what is today Buenos Aires before traveling up the Paraná River to Paraguay, where he deployed the majority of his resources.

The Spanish founded settlements hither, thither, and yon, but their impulse was to expand the Crown's territorial claims, not to develop them economically for the sake of their new inhabitants. They left future generations to concern themselves with how these scattered settlements could be connected to each other and to the larger world, the civilized world, of which they were the remotest offshoots. Our forefathers on this continent focused their efforts on adapting themselves to the new environment in which they found themselves. For them, connections to each other and the larger world would depend for centuries on hoofed animals. They learned to recognize the finest tracks of hooved animals in the bone-dry earth. Expert pathfinders known as "*baqueanos*" became the most revered of wise men. As they stopped being Spaniards to become *criollos*, they abandoned trousers in favor of garments like the Guaraní chiripá.[2] Without the materials necessary to make Spanish-style saddles,

---

2. The chiripá is a garment historically worn by men of Indigenous origin and later became a standard element in gaucho dress.

5. Civilization in Daily Life

our forefathers learned to ride their horses using a sheep-fleece "recado." Instead of European-style shoes, they shod their feet with rawhide taken from a colt's hind legs.

The great distances that separated cities and forts from one another also separated Spanish settlers from the cities and forts. In a land characterized by great distances, horses defined the patterns of human movement and mediated virtually all activities. Argentina became the real-life location of a classical fantasy, a primitive land of centaurs, half human and half horse. This dependence on the horse has exercised a destructive influence on the social organization of our country, contributing to the backwardness and barbarism against which we continue to struggle. In the unpeopled land of great distances, horsemen have all the power and prestige. That is the heart of the issue. Thirty years of Rosista tyranny, half a century of civil war fueled by imperishable, petty hatreds—the ultimate cause of this catastrophe lies in the vast open spaces that make men on horseback the arbiters of our political life. The war heroes and caudillos who hold sway over us are always and exclusively men on horseback. A tyrant may rule on foot, but a caudillo must rule on horseback. In fact, to mobilize his followers for a military campaign, the caudillo's traditional message is simply: *estoy a caballo*—I've mounted up.

And now, gentlemen, the railroad has come to put an end to the horseman's dominion over us. The railroad conquers the distances that gave him that dominion, and it does so more thoroughly than horses ever could. Fast, safe railroads will now connect isolated communities to each other and rapidly extend the civilizing influence of large cities, with their arts, culture, and refinements. Advancing science, trade, and political liberty will accompany the new, iron horse everywhere it goes. The cheerful puffing of the locomotive will represent, to every ear, the sound of progress.

Railroads have done more than political revolutions to advance human progress. Eventually, railroads will lead to the disappearance of national borders, just as they have already vastly increased freedom of movement within nations. A railroad car, bringing together travelers of all ages and social classes, is a great leveler. The haughty magnate that once rode alone in his elegant carriage, splashing pedestrians in the muddy street, now must fraternize with the common people in a common conveyance, and the commoners themselves can gain a nodding acquaintance with the superior manners and decorum of their social superiors, merely by traveling in a railroad car. Our simple countrymen can now experience, if only for an hour or two, the dignity of our sophisticated urban culture in

5. Civilization in Daily Life

the presence of both men and women. Not a few will desire more polish for themselves. Their aspirations will alter in many cases, and along with their aspirations, their clothing and their speech, although that can only occur more gradually.

To build railroads is to recover the ground that Buenos Aires lost to barbarism during our first half century of nationhood. The outlying hamlets of Belgrano, San Isidro, and San Fernando will become, within a few years, what San Martín and Morón have already become—neighborhoods integrated into the metropolis, bedroom communities, suppliers of vegetables and milk to the entire urban population, facilitating its further growth. To strengthen the internal communications of our nation is, overall, to facilitate all sorts of sharing and exchange, and that is the basis of all social development. Self-sufficiency may enable survival, but it leads inexorably to social isolation and poverty. Without access to an extensive market for their trade, towns will never develop into cities. Three centuries after their founding, remote towns of the Argentine interior such as San Luis, La Rioja, and Santiago del Estero seem stuck in time, where each passing generation bequeaths only destitution, ignorance, and obscurantism to the next. The railroad whose construction we inaugurate today will reinvigorate countless sleepy hamlets and give them a new reason to exist.

Of special importance will be rail connection to a number of river ports such as San Fernando and El Tigre. The navigation of the great Paraná River, the traditional avenue of exportation for the products of Argentina's tropical north and Paraguay, must be the indispensable complement to our emerging railway network. The wide estuary of Río de la Plata, by the time it reaches the port of Buenos Aires, is too stormy and turbulent for riverboats. Modern steam-driven riverboats, such as those that operate on the Mississippi or Hudson Rivers, are practically floating palaces, several stories tall. With their shallow draft and tall superstructure, such craft are vulnerable to maritime gale-force winds. Because they cannot safely access the port of Buenos Aires, such craft have not yet begun to operate on the Paraná. When it reaches San Fernando, our new railroad will have connected Buenos Aires to a Paraná port accessible to modern steam-powered riverboats. The result will be to connect our interior and exterior trade circuits, a momentous advance in the national integration of Argentina.

Only a few days ago, word arrived from Corrientes concerning an enormous raft of cedar logs that had been cut along the banks of the Bermejo River and assembled at Oran, the first-ever shipment of the kind.

5. Civilization in Daily Life

Rail connection between a serviceable river port and Buenos Aires will facilitate shipments of the most varied resources from the provinces of our tropical north and Paraguay. In addition, it will enable access by the urban population to the islands of the Paraná delta, nearby our bustling capital and ideally located to offer it provisions and recreation.

The future of our country provides limitless scope for my remarks today, but I won't try the patience of my listeners. Let us look confidently beyond current events to build a better future. Today we sow the seeds of progress in fertile ground before returning to more immediate concerns. By planting the seeds of progress, we show ourselves to be enlightened, patriotic citizens worthy of a free country. No less than our intrepid national guards, we are contributing to the advance of civilization and the defeat of barbarism.

Today, the railroad to San Fernando is no longer merely a fond dream. Today, it begins to be a reality. Only yesterday, news arrived from London confirming the company's intention to complete this project as soon as sufficient capital becomes available. The legal framework has been established, the furrow lies open, the seed has been planted, and the work has begun. May the swift success of this project stimulate many, many more! Let these rails extend to Rosario, to Córdoba, to Tucumán, eventually allowing all Argentines to share a fraternal embrace!

Godspeed, San Fernando Railroad!

Obras, vol. 21, 116–21

"Rustic Capital,"
Annals of Education, 1858

If some sudden, revolutionary change eliminated the circulation of paper money, the Argentine gaucho would be only slightly incommoded. He would simply use some of the silver coins that traditionally decorate and occupy pockets of his wide belt, his *tirador*. The capital so deposited would go a long way toward supplying this country's need for circulating specie. How did our gauchos accumulate such wealth into their daily apparel?

Although we've never had the silver mines of Chile, Mexico, or Peru, no other entire country in the Americas consumes more silver than does

5. Civilization in Daily Life

Buenos Aires, city and countryside. La Calle del Buen Orden, getting to the outskirts of the city, and several other streets, such as Lomilleros, where the manufacturers of local riding gear cluster—these are the locations of many silversmiths, their displays overflowing with a sparkling sea of silver ornaments for a horse's saddle and bridle, not to mention silver spurs, silver-handled riding crops, forms of ostentation of which our gauchos are inordinately fond. An excessive proliferation of silver on the cheek and crown pieces of some horse's bridles had the effect of lowering their heads, the topic of some commentary among knowledgeable observers. I consulted a silversmith who assured me that the whole set, not including a pure silver bit, which is an unusual height of ostentation, runs in the neighborhood of six to eight thousand pesos.

Moreover, our countrymen like their silver coined. Prestigious mintages sell for far more than their value by weight. The coins are used decoratively and, though this may appear surprising, they are melted down to make other objects, most particularly spurs. One manufacturer of silver items for equestrian ostentation recently bought one thousand silver marks for that purpose. Sometimes a gaucho will acquire coins, one by one, paying above its value by weight for each of them, over a considerable period of time, in order to have them melted and made into silver spurs. The precipitous mintage, in his eyes, is a guarantee of quality. That is why gauchos tend to spurn imitations fashioned of cheaper materials and reject in horror the idea of silver plating. Appearances seem to matter less than the gaucho's own confidence in the true value of his possessions.

These customs may appear quaint, but they have a rhyme and reason that apply in many countries with similar traditional ways of life. One could say that the same coins our gauchos carry at their waists, Oriental women carry braided into their tresses. Egyptian mamelukes likewise carry all their wealth in the adornment of their persons, their weapons, and their saddles and bridles. Following the battle of the pyramids, in which Napoleon's forces decimated the mameluke defenders, the French spent several days collecting gems and precious metals from the cadavers of their slain enemies. The chronic insecurity of an ambulatory way of life recommends maintaining wealth under the watchful eye and permanent armed guard of the owner himself. Such customs therefore often characterize pastoral cultures.

Thus, the apparent whimsy and extravagance of the gaucho's tirador is better understood, more prosaically, as a primitive savings account. True, his savings account is inferior to the modern variety because a horseman's tirador is obviously more vulnerable to robbery than a bank vault

5. Civilization in Daily Life

and, also, because the gaucho's deposits there earn him no interest. And yet, as a traditional sort of savings, this custom of our rural population demonstrates an important virtue. Because of it, the country people of Chile or Bolivia have a much lower standard of living than ours. They are more likely than our gauchos to spend all their earnings on drink. Their savings start from scratch every Monday, so to speak, and never survive the weekend. Their ragged clothing contrasts with the gaucho's impeccable costume. Their lack of forethought and long-term planning contrasts with the gaucho's patient accumulation of silver coins. The gaucho takes care to determine the intrinsic worth of his small extravagances, and then he wears it on his sleeve, one could say, thereby staking a claim to monetary substance and social respectability.

Subtle distinctions in wealth are visibly expressed in this way. In addition to his tirador covered with coins, no gaucho is without a knife for use in everything from working to eating to fighting, but not all knives have a silver handle and scabbard. At the next level up, the gaucho of somewhat higher wealth will signal that fact by acquiring heavy silver spurs. Silver adornments on the bridle and other accessories—including riding crops and even the hobble used to keep the horse from straying while it grazes—can be added to signal further advances in wealth and prestige. The number of rural men engaged in this process of capital accumulation must be fairly large, to judge by the thousands of expensive pieces on sale in the mentioned areas of Buenos Aires.

What a shame that the overconfident young deputies of our legislature recently delayed plans to collect all that peripatetic capital in our national bank. The countryside of Argentina literally sparkles with unproductive capital. Many countrymen will no doubt eagerly deposit their silver treasure in specialized bank branches, relieved of the necessity of perpetually guarding it, and come away carrying only a receipt, as long as they are confident of their ability to recover their treasure at any time. Our bank branch at San Nicolás had already commenced the great task of putting our sparkling but unproductive rural capital to work. One third to one half of that bank's current paper emissions of ten million pesos represents silver that emerged from countless tiradores and from melting down countless spurs and bridle ornaments. Neither spurs nor tiradores are worn in the city, after all.

Further from Buenos Aires, the news is hardly out. Until recently, our simple rural people haven't known about banks. They haven't understood that the silver of their spurs and bridles would be employed far more efficiently if melted down and deposited safely in a bank, where it would earn something called interest. For them, this is a suspicious initiative of city people. And our country people mistrust city people, like the peddlers who emerge from the city to cheat them in any way possible. They don't understand that having more liquid capital would free them from those bloodsuckers.

Yet today, our Argentine countrymen are participating in the same phenomena that affect the entire civilized world. They have a new interest in saving for their children's education. Right now, they still put their savings in the tirador. It's not their fault if the more intelligent part of society has been remiss in teaching them better. One could describe for them the example of the US state of Massachusetts. It maintains savings accounts in the amount of 33,000,000 pesos, belonging to 150,000 depositors. You won't find the head of a family in the state who isn't busy earning interest and contributing, by his savings, to the economic development of Massachusetts. Of course, almost without exception, the men of Massachusetts have received a good public education, and there is nothing like schooling to awaken people's aspirations and, thus, a desire to save. With education or without it, the era of silver spurs is coming to an end. Modern European-style saddles as well as changes of clothing styles in rural areas are making silver ornaments and tiradores a thing of the past. It won't be long before the only place to see such items will be in a museum of costly antique curiosities. It won't be long now before the gaucho reaches habitually, not for his tirador, but for his gold timepiece. In that bright and not-so-distant future, time will have become money, giving a gold watch and chain the symbolic importance once attached to silver spurs. Thus did Texas cowboys put aside their own silver accouterments under the influence of US industrialism.

Finally, what about silver-plated objects? In gathering and issuing paper currency to represent the vast profusion of silver objects and ornaments, how can we assure the quality of the silver? Some spurs, buttons, and bridle pieces are solid silver, and some small percentage—difficult to detect in that vast profusion of objects—are silver-plated. A quick and efficient way to tell the difference is not yet available. For now it is probably best to begin the enormous task of receiving the sparkling but unproductive capital of our countryside into bank deposits. As our countrymen gain confidence in the security of their deposits and become more attentive to the idea of interest, the silver will come flooding in.

Obras, vol. 42, pp. 36–40

5. Civilization in Daily Life
"Educating Women"

The future annals of our current international Pedagogical Congress, the first ever to convene in South America, will honor the name of Clementina C. de Alió. This distinguished lady has made herself a tribune to argue with enlightened reason and appropriate emotion for the importance of women's employment and educational opportunities. She has argued, moreover, that providing wider opportunities for women benefits not only the women, but rather constitutes a fundamental foundation of improvement, overall, for the common people of Argentina.

For sociologists, her argument seems a self-evident truth, but it's a truth that few of us have absorbed. In the words of a French analyst, "The state has an enormous, and enormously underappreciated, interest in educating women, which it systematically neglects to do. Educating women benefits all people, because women educate everyone else, most especially in the critical early years of life. Our early education (informal, of course, but no less powerful therefore) begins, in fact, when infants begin to learn by imitation, and their principal instructors are their mothers. When we begin school, we don't yet know any Latin or Greek, any history or geography. Yet our characters have been mostly shaped already. Our notions of truth and falsehood, of spirituality and religion, our virtues and vices, our reactions of tolerance or anger—these things we have by that time already learned from the woman who raised us." Schooling women today, concludes Monsieur Legouvé, raises the future educational level of those societies more effectively than any other single measure. Our own Señora de Alió makes a similar point with admirable precision and clarity when she says that "nature, by making women mothers, made them educators," and that, by "educating mothers, one educates their children as well." This point should stand as axiomatic from now on. Educating women is an urgent obligation of the state because women provide the fundamental preschool basis for all formal schooling of both men and women.

Children's preschool education continues, more formalized, in primary school, and the Señora de Alió has shown conclusively that primary schooling, too, should be done by women. "Primary schools should be in women's hands," she says, "so that children find them to be an extension of their nurturing and educational home life, offering similar care and affection. Women's role as primary caregiver for children in the home fits them for that same role as teachers in the first years of school. This was nature's educational design, and it should be ours." The current

5. Civilization in Daily Life

international Pedagogical Congress should thoroughly consider these recommendations of Clementina C. de Alió and incorporate them into their formal resolutions.

The estimable Señora de Alió has words as well concerning the social redemption and moral salvation of women through honest toil. On this point, whether or not she is aware of it, she has distinguished predecessors in the Río de la Plata. I refer to founding fathers Manuel Belgrano and Bernardino Rivadavia. In 1796, Belgrano lamented the social condition of women and the miserable conditions of life that drove some into prostitution. He proposed the creation of new opportunities for humble women to engage in honest labor, and he concurred with more recent authorities concerning their "ripple effects," writing that "reforms aimed at bettering the feminine condition will improve the moral health of the whole society." As for President Rivadavia, in his address inaugurating the Women's Beneficent Society in April 1823 he specified that one of society's goals was to teach "industrial arts." He indicated "that women ought to take over tasks suitable to their talents, even those normally accomplished by men, so that the latter may concentrate exclusively on activities requiring the application of masculine strength." Rivadavia believed that a woman's education should provide her with the means to provide for herself through her own labor, independently of men's support. The idea that women are inherently incapable of supporting themselves, wrote Rivadavia, "should be spiritedly and absolutely rejected."

These advanced ideas thus appeared quite early here in Buenos Aires, and yet since the independence period there have been few echoes of them, even now that the world's most advanced nations, which we ought to adopt as models for ourselves, are putting those ideas into practice. And now the distinguished Señora de Alió, who has no reason to have read Belgrano's report or Rivadavia's address from so many years ago, has put these ideas on the table at the current international Pedagogical Congress. It is remarkable that through her purity of sentiment and clarity of thought, she has recreated the noble impulses that stirred the foundation of our republic.

Good ideas never die. They only disappear from the surface of human affairs for a while, perhaps repressed and pushed into the murky depths. Then, when opportune conditions for their development reappear, the good ideas reemerge in the sunlight, like seeds planted long before, to luxuriate, bloom, and put forth fruit. So, let us attend to the resolutions of the Pedagogical Congress, trusting that it will embrace the gospel of the Señora de Alió—not to mention Belgrano and Rivadavia—and explain how the seeds planted on our shores more than half a century ago can finally grow strong and provide their superb fruit to nourish the Argentine nation.

Obras, vol. 48, pp. 130–32

Selection from "North and South America. A Discourse Delivered before the Rhode-Island Historical Society," 27 December 1865[3]

In America, the United States have succeeded by means of an internal social war, in taking a definitive position in the political world, passing from an attempt at institutions to an initial civilization, armed at all points, and in order to serve as a rule and model, necessarily prepared for one of those general conclusions on which humanity is anxious to repose after each one of its fractions has maintained some separate truth.

More space and meditation would be necessary than that which an introductory address admits, in order to determine . . . what are the elements which constitute North American civilization. We will indicate those which enter into our purpose—Intellectual aptitude generalized for the whole nation and for all generations, by a plan of universal education, so as to appropriate to itself every new progress of human knowledge in all countries. Preparation of the soil determined by railroads, canals, rivers, and seas to a rapid movement and circulation; and all this conjunction of natural and acquired advantages, impelled and governed by a system of political instruction which has the sanction of time, of fruitful and happy experience, and what is more, the moral sanction of the human conscience in all countries, supposing that the right to civil and religious liberty of action and thought is indeed an unquestionable truth in the conscience of men.

---

3. As the Argentine minister to the United States, Sarmiento delivered this speech, which was published in English (translator unknown) in 1866 in Providence, RI, by Knowles, Anthony & Co. This excerpt (pp. 29; 43–44) gives a sense of what is a much longer and more detailed comparison of civilization and links to national and international success in North and South America. Note in particular the emphasis Sarmiento places on education.

5. Civilization in Daily Life

As may be seen by this address, none of the actual powers of the earth holds in its bosom or in its essence, all . . . of these elements of present greatness and of future development.

On the other side, only England and the United States have fundamental institutions to offer as models to the future world. England because she propagates hers with her commerce, industry, and language, to her numerous colonies, not exporting from her own territory her monarchy or her nobility; the United States because they have fertilized and diffused them upon their own territory which is exempted from the traditions of the past. Aristocratic England may be proud of having produced the democratic United States, as the patrician Cornelia was proud of her Gracchi of the Tribune; but she fails to see whether the modern Gracchi understand better how to direct the popular forces, and saving themselves from themselves, save the world from one of those retrogressions which follow the wanderings of the initiators.

Man does not live by bread alone; and we have New-England to prove it for the honor of the human race, and in compliance with the precept, I have already shown you how the spirit of Horace Mann colonized South America, raising excellent schools wherever his doctrines are known. This moral action should be continued, spread abroad, strengthened. . . .

In the schools which I have visited [across the United States], French is taught in some, German in others, Spanish in none. Are your teachers preparing to go to France to teach the principles of American liberty? The Spanish language is the key to South America. Your great historians owe to it their fame; your navigators, engineers, and builders require it whenever they travel; on either side of Cape Horn, from California to Havana, their vessels touch the coast or penetrate to the interior. In the olden time, when nations looked back into the past while advancing, the Greeks learned the Egyptian language, the Romans learned Greek, the barbarians Latin. They feared to go astray. Now, however, that the nations are self-reliant and progressive, it is the language of the future which they should learn, and English is the language of the oceanic world, as Spanish is the language destined to spread itself in continuity with English throughout the vast extent of South America. The Castilian language lies before the North American people like a conducting wire, and should be the language taught in the schools where any other language is taught besides English.

6. Sarmiento the National Hero

At Sarmiento's funeral in September 1888, Argentina's vice president, Carlos Pellegrini (soon to be president), gave an expected laudatory oration. What stands out, though, is how Pellegrini ended the speech: recognizing Sarmiento, with the full force of the Argentine state behind his claim, as one of Argentina's father figures, "from now on and forever."

As the coda to this collection of Sarmiento's writings, one might reflect on the areas of Sarmiento's influence that Pellegrini highlights—the areas where his legacy could endure—and the points of connection with selections throughout this volume.

❋ ❋ ❋

Funerary Honors for Sarmiento, 21 September 1888

Eulogy by Vice President Dr. Don Carlos Pellegrini

Mr. President, Gentlemen:

After the last and supreme struggle, Sarmiento now shuffles off this mortal coil, like some mythic warrior of antiquity, after the last rude combat, letting fall his sword, beaten at last by dint of overwhelming force. But his glory remains. All men bow down to it. Even the tents of his warlike adversaries have fallen silent. The flags have been lowered, covered. The drummers drum a single-noted dirge.

6. Sarmiento the National Hero

All Buenos Aires knows Sarmiento by sight, or knew him, as the highest of peaks in South America—the sun glinting off his proud, snow-capped brow, his deep interior trembling with volcanic thunder. Living with him close up sometimes made it difficult to appreciate the vastness of his significance as a public figure. Now that the colossus has crashed to earth, so to speak, its titanic granite and marble fragments, scattered over half a continent and half a century of our American history, make that vastness manifest. Each fragment could become a monument: granite for towers and battlements, finest marble for the sculptor's art. Such a colossus was Sarmiento.

He was an original, not the expression of a social milieu, not the product of his age. He was, in fact, the most powerful thinker to emerge so far in our America, and the greatest statesman. A condor that soared over the Andes, he would have excelled in any place or time. Born a century ago, he would have been a founder of the Argentine Republic, more important than Moreno, on a par with Rivadavia. Instead Sarmiento was born in the year that our protracted struggle for independence began, and it was he who saw, better than anyone else, how to achieve our national destiny. All along the winding road to where we stand today, he has carried the brightest of the many beacons that have guided our footsteps.

Writer, orator, legislator, minister, president, his labors were vast and continuous. For his political creed, he was an apostle and a soldier.

His country was the same immense and wild patrimony inherited by all his generation. He devoted himself, with all his soul, to its betterment, principally by carving paths through the forest of ignorance giving us access to civilization, broad paths that have since been well trodden. We saw him in the guise of a sweaty North American–style pioneer, his eyes bright with a vision of transformation, his sharp ax poised to chop away at the barbaric thicket of wilderness, opening always toward the pleasant groves of civilization. Encountering, planted in his path, the Tree of Tyranny, we saw him spring forward without hesitation to wield his sharp ax again, without rest or interruption of any kind, against its knurly trunk, until down it came, opening a vast stretch of luminous, starry sky in the forest of ignorance, allowing us to gaze up at last, and dream.

His was a life of action and of struggle. He possessed, in his personal arsenal, every weapon imaginable. But his herculean intelligence was the greatest of them, like a medieval warrior's mace, capable of smashing the solidest defense to smithereens.

He was ever the same, in all situations, whether as chief executive, or senator, or private citizen in his own hearth and home, ever spontaneous,

6. Sarmiento the National Hero

witty, thoughtful, oblivious to anything petty or mean or ridiculous, his integrity unbending, his energy and tenacity inexhaustible.

He lacked the power to seduce the masses, the charm enjoyed by many political leaders who engender great popularity. Intelligence, rather than sentiment, was always his lodestar. At times he might not inspire affection among the common people, but always, without exception, he commanded their admiration and respect.

In Congress his bench was regarded by his colleagues as the seat of a chaired professor. Whenever his voice was heard in that august body, all present lent an attentive ear. His eloquence might be stormy, full of thunder and lightning when passionate, but never childish or vulgar, always radiant, by the end, with clarity and enlightenment.

Our progress as a nation owes incalculably much to Sarmiento. His lifetime of labor plowed the virgin soil of Argentina, sowing the seeds of future greatness at every step. A few seeds may have fallen on rocky ground, but most took root, and today the crops that he planted stand tall. They have made us who we are today. Our undying gratitude to the plowman!

Did he make mistakes, commit an occasional injustice? Possibly. I can't confirm that he did not. "The evil that men do lives after them; the good is oft interred with their bones," wrote Shakespeare in reference to Julius Caesar. Let it not be so with Sarmiento.

Today, on his last day on earth, as we follow his mortal remains to their eternal resting place, let our schoolchildren gather to throw flowers in his final path. Their voices, together, the voice of the future, rise together in homage to the fervent architect of Argentine public education.

Today, the public schools that he created stand in every town and village of our republic, and there they will remain, as winking beacons in the evening sky, now that the sun has descended at last to the horizon.

In the name of the Senate that he served in life, I deposit our collective tribute of admiration and respect before his casket. Now he belongs to the ages. And when our Argentine Republic eventually takes its place at last among the leading nations of the globe, its sons and daughters can look back at those winking stars in the firmament and recognize there the profile of Sarmiento, consecrated now for all time as a Founding Father.

INDEX

Bold page numbers indicate an image.

Alberdi, Juan Bautista, xix, 58
Alió, Clementina C. de, 100–101
Alsina, Adolfo, xxii, 66, 69–70
Andrade, Olegario, 51
Angelis, Pedro de, 44
Argentina, **xxxiv**; civilization and barbarism in, 4, 8, 27–28; cost of living, 59, 64; Europe and, 3, 7–8, 10–11, 14–15, 43; Federal–Unitarian division, xv–xvi, xviii–xix, 37, 39–41; immigration to, ix–x, xxv–xxvi, 9, 58–65; independence of, xiii–xiv, 27, 105; Indigenous population, xxiv–xxv, 9, 65–70; judges in, 26–27; musical inclination, 16–17; national character, 13, 13n5, 14–23; physical geography of, 5–15; power in, xv–xxi, 26–28; public education in, xxv–xxvi, 75; religious life in, 12–13; Rivadavia and, xiv–xv; rural life in, 9–15, 27–28, 61–64; Spanish colonization, xv, 4, 7, 9, 20, 57, 93–94. *See also* Buenos Aires
Argentine Confederation, xix, xxi, 55
Artigas, José Gervasio, 27, 57
Avellaneda, Nicolás, viii, xxiv

barbarism: caudillos and, ix, xvi, 37; Christmas Eve celebrations, 81–83; El Chacho and, 52–54; Facundo Quiroga and, 3–4, 31–36; gauchos and, xvi, 22; Indians and, 28, 54–55, 66–67; Latin American dichotomy, viii–ix; rural life and, 7, 10, 13–14, 27–28, 51. *See also* civilization
Barros Arana, Diego, 44
Belgrano, Manuel, 101
Bolívar, Simón, xiv
Brazil, xiv–xv, xviii, xx–xxii, 20
Bretón de los Herreros, Manuel, 84–85
Buenos Aires: autonomous state of, xxi, xxv; Carnival in, 88–92; conformity in, 40–41; Federal party and, 39–40, 50; gaucho resistance, 38; immigrants in, 9, 59–61; interprovincial Congress, xiv; organized settlement projects, 62; physical geography of, 7–8; political power and, 27; railroad to San Fernando, 93–96; red ribbon in, 39–41, 50; regime terrorism in, 40–41, 46–49; trade blockade, xx

Calfurucá, 66, 68–69
Calíbar, 18–19
Cambaceres, Antonio, 70
Camila, 42
Carnival, 86–92

Index

Catholicism, xv–xxvi, 12–13, 81, 86
Catriel, 65, 69
caudillos: barbarism and, ix, xvi, 37; Federal party and, xvi–xviii, xxi, xxvi, 37; gaucho followers, xvi–xxiv; horses and, 94; political power, xvii–xviii, 27, 52, 55; rebellions, xxiii–xxiv
Chacho's rebellion, xxi
Chaco, xxiii–xxiv, 6
Chamosa, Oscar, viii, x, xiii
Chile: cultural criticism, 79–80; Facundo Quiroga and, 32; independence movement, xiii–xiv; newspaper readership, 2, 47, 76, 76n1, 79; publication of *Facundo*, viii, 2, 42–43; Sarmiento exile to, xvi, xviii–xix, 1, 4, 43, 76n1; theater in, 84–85
Christmas Eve celebrations, 80–83
citizenship, 70–74
civilization: banking and, 98–99; biological explanations, xxv, 30; Carnival and, 91–92; caudillos and, ix, xvi; education and, 102; immigration and, 58; Latin American dichotomy, viii–ix; newspaper readership, 75–80; possession of land, 14–15, 62–64; railroads and, 93–96; Sarmiento on, 1, 3–4, 8–9, 14, 51; society and, 11, 22, 27; urban vs. rural, viii, 1, 4, 13–14, 51, 75. *See also* barbarism
Cooper, James Fenimore, xvi, 14–15, 57, 66
Córdoba: caudillos and, xvii–xviii; gauchos, 38, 53;
Mapuche confederation and, xxiv; physical geography of, 7–8; populations in, 9–10; support for Sarmiento in, xxii cultural criticism, 79–80

Derquí, Santiago, 53, 53n1
Dumas, Alexandre, 84

Echeverría, Esteban, xix, 15–16
El Chacho, ix, xxi, xxiii, 24, 51–57
El Progreso, 43
Entre Ríos, xvii, xx, xxii–xxiv, xxvii, 55
estancieros, xv, xvi
Europe: Argentina and, 3, 7–8, 10–11, 14–15, 43; citizenship in, 71; civilization and, viii, 1, 4, 8, 13–14, 28, 36; immigration from, xxv–xxvi, 9, 58–59, 61–65; impact of *Facundo*, viii, 42–43; Rosas resistance to, xx; Sarmiento travels in, xix; theater in, 84

Federalists (*Federales*): caudillos alliance, xvi–xviii, xxi, xxvi, 37; domination of Argentine Republic, 37; Mazorca violence, 40; provincial rights, xv; Quiroga and, xviii, 37–38; Rosas and, 39–41, 50
Fortoul, Hippolyte, 1, 1n1

gauchos: barbarism and, xvi, 22; caudillos and, xvi, xxiii–xxiv; gaucho malo, 20–21, 23, 26; horsemanship, 21–22, 24, 26; knife fighting, 25–26, 29, 33;

108

Index

military commanders for, 27; *montoneras*, 28, 28n7, 34–35; musical inclination, 16–17; pathfinders, 20, 23, 28; poetic sensibility, 16–17; provincialism, 38; *pulpería*, 23–28; rebellions, xxi, xxiii–xxiv; rural life and, 11–15; superstition and, 15–16; *tirador*, 96–99; trackers, 17–19, 28; troubadour/cantor, 22–23, 28; vagrancy laws and, 33; violent death and, 13–14, 23, 25
Generation of 1837, xix, xxi
Gutiérrez, Eduardo, xvi
Gutiérrez, Ladislao, 48–50

Hamilton, Alexander, vii, xiii
Hernández, José, xvi, 51
Hudson, W. H., xvi
Hugo, Victor, 24, 84

immigration: agricultural labor, 62–64; civilization and, 58; economic activity, 60–63; European, xxv–xxvi, 9, 58–59, 61–64; moral character and, ix, 60–61; naturalization, 70–74; organized settlement projects, 62–65
Indigenous people/Indians: barbarism and, 28, 54–55, 66–67; eradication of, xxiii–xxv, 65–70; rural life and, 9; southeastern frontier, 70; *vidalita* and, 16

landscape: Americas and, 6, 14–15; immensity and, 6, 15; pampas, 15, 22; physical geography of, 6, 8; poetic response, 14–16, 45; power and, xvi–xvii, 4
La Rioja province, xvii–xviii, xxiii, 38
Larra, Mariano José de, 84–85
Latin America, viii–x, xv, xxv, **xxxiii**, 75
Longfellow, Henry Wadsworth, xix
López, Estanislao, xvii
López, Francisco Solano, xxi
López Jordán, Ricardo, xxiv

Mann, Horace, xix, 45, 103
Mann, Mary, xix, xxii, 45
Mapuche confederation, xxiv–xxv
Martí, José, viii
Maspero, Gaston, 45
Mercantile Gazette, The, 43
Miranda, Lin Manuel, vii, xiii
Mitre, Bartolomé, xxi–xxiii
Murder of Camila O'Gorman, The, 46, 48
music, 16–17

Namuncurá, 65, 69
newspapers: in Buenos Aires, 47; Chilean, 2, 47, 76, 76n1, 79; civilization and, 75–80; cultural criticism, 79–80; readership of, 76–79; Sarmiento writing in, ix, xiii, xix, 42, 76n1; in the United States, 77

O'Gorman, Camila, 42, 45–50
Ontivero, 55–57
organized settlement projects, 62–65

Index

Paraguay, xiv, xx–xxiii, 95–96
Pedro I, xiv
Pedro II, xx
Pellegrini, Carlos, 104
Peñaloza, Ángel Vicente. *See* El Chacho
Perón, Eva, xxvi
Perón, Juan, xxvi
phrenology, 30, 30n9, 31
Pincen, 65
poetry, 14–17, 45
public education: in Argentina, xxv–xxvi; civilization and, 102–3; nonwhites, xxv–xxvi; Sarmiento on, xiii, xix, xxii, xxv–xxvii, 75, 103; in the United States, xix, 99, 103; women and, 100–102
pulpería, 23–28

Quiroga, Juan Facundo: animosity towards veterans, 34; atavism and, 54; barbarism and, 3–4, 31–36; character of, 30–31, 35–36; construction of *tapias*, 32; control of La Rioja, 38; death of, xviii–xix, 2, 52; Federal party and, xviii, 37–38; gambling, 32–34, 36; knife fighting, 33–34; life of, 28–37; *montonera* of, 34–35, 57; pretense of psychic powers, 35–37; Rosas alliance, 38–39; rural power and, 28; violence by, 33–36. *See also* Sarmiento, Domingo Faustino. *Facundo*

railroads, 93–96
Ramírez, Francisco, xvii, 34–35
Reinafé brothers, xviii

Revue des Deux Mondes, 43, 45
Río de la Plata, xiii–xv, xxi–xxii, 6–7, 95
Rivadavia, Bernardino, xiv–xv, xviii, 101
Rivera, Fructuoso, 20
Roca, Julio A., xxiv, xxv, 66–67
Rosas, Juan Manuel de: animosity towards veterans, 34; defeat of, xxi, xxiv; execution of O'Gorman and Gutiérrez, 47–50; Federal party and, 39–41; immigration and, 58; as pathfinder, 20; political power, xvii–xx, 38–40; protection of killers, 25–26; Sarmiento on, viii–ix, 3–4, 8; trade blockade, xx; tyranny of, 3–4, 8, 39–42
Rugendas, Johann Moritz, 43, 43n1
rural life: barbarism and, 7, 10, 13–14, 27–28, 51; capital in, 96–99; Catholicism in, 12–13; education and, 12–13; horses and, 24, 26; Indigenous people, 9; judges in, 26–27; leadership and, 26–28; livestock raising, 10–12, 14, 24, 62; military commanders, 27; musical inclination, 16; pathfinders, 19–20, 23; physical geography and, 5–15; poetic response, 15–16; *pulpería*, 23–28; social life and, 11–12; subsistence agriculture, 63–64; trackers, 17–19; troubadour/cantor, 22–23; violent death and, 6, 13–14; women's domestic work, 12, 24. *See also* gauchos

Index

San Fernando, 93–96
San Juan River valley, xvii, xxvi, 53
San Martín, José de, xiii–xiv, 35
Santa Fe, 62–64
Sarmiento, Domingo Faustino: on Camila O'Gorman, 45–50; on Carnival, 86–92; on caudillos, ix, xxiii, xxvii; on Christmas Eve celebrations, 80–83; on citizenship rights, 70–74; civilization and barbarism, xxvi–xxvii, 4, 51, 75; on cultural criticism, 79–80; death of, xxvii, 104; early life, vii, xiii–xv, xvii; on education of women, 100–102; exile in Chile, xvi, xviii–xix, 1, 4, 43, 76n1; funerary honors for, 104–6; on immigration, ix, 58–61; impact in Argentina, vii–xxvii; on Indians, 65–70; Mapuche confederation and, xxiv; on organized settlement projects, 62–65; presidency of, xiii, xv, xxii–xxv; public education and, xiii, xix, xxii, xxv, xxvii, 75, 103; on railroad, 93–96; on rural capital, 96–99; San Juan governor, xxi, xxiii, 51; on theater, 83–86; travel to the United States, xix–xx, xxii–xxiii, 102, 102n3; Unitarian army, xviii; writings of, vii–x, xiii, xix
Sarmiento, Domingo Faustino. *El Chacho: The Last Caudillo of the Llanos*: atavism and, 54–55; El Chacho followers, 52–56; Indigenous tradition, 54–55; Ontivero in, 55–57; rural barbarism, 51–57; violence and, 53–56
Sarmiento, Domingo Faustino. *Facundo*: Argentine character, 13, 13n5, 14–23; barbarism of Quiroga, 30–35; caudillos in, ix, xvi; civilization-barbarism in, 1, 3–4, 7–12, 14, 27–28; on gauchos, 11–29; influence of, viii–ix, 42–43; on judges, 26–27; landscape in, 6, 8, 14–15; on life of Quiroga, 28–37; on military commanders, 27; on phrenology, 30–31; physical geography of Argentina, 5–15; on political power, 26–27; on *pulpería*, 23–28; reception of, 42–45; religious life in, 12–13; on Rosas, 20, 25–26; on Rosas tyranny, xix, 3–4, 8, 38–42; rural life in, 9–28; Spanish and Indian populations, 9–10; translations of, 43–45
Sarmiento, Domingo Faustino. Works of: *Annals of Education*, 96; *Conflicts and Harmony among Races in the Americas*, xxv; *Crónica*, 45; *El Diario*, 70; *El Mercurio*, 76, 76n1, 79–80, 83, 86; *El Nacional*, 43–44, 58, 62, 65, 67; *Life of Dominguito*, xxii; *Life of Lincoln*, xxii; *North and South America*, 102; *Recuerdos de Provincia*, 42–43
Sarmiento, Domingo Fidel, xxii–xxiii
Scott, Walter, xvi, 45, 89
Sucre, José Antonio de, xiv

theater, 83–86, 91–92
Tocqueville, Alexis de, xx

Unitarians (*Unitarios*), xv–xvi, xviii, 37, 40
United Provinces of the Río de la Plata, xiii, xv
United States: banking in, 99; civilization and, 102; cost of living, 59; immigration to, 59, 71; impact of *Facundo*, viii; newspaper readership, 77; public education in, xix, 99, 103; Sarmiento travels in, xix–xx, xxii–xxiii
Urquiza, Justo José de, xx–xxii, xxiv

Varela, Felipe, xxiii–xxiv

War of Independence, xiv
women: Carnival and, 86–90; domestic work, 12, 24; education of, 100–102; gaucho malos, 21; guitar serenades, 16–17